The First Americans

TIME
LIFE
BOOKS

The Emergence of Man

The First Americans

by Robert Claiborne
and the Editors
of TIME-LIFE BOOKS

TIME-LIFE INTERNATIONAL
Nederland B.V.

The Author: ROBERT CLAIBORNE, formerly an Editor on the staff of TIME-LIFE BOOKS, writes primarily in the fields of medicine and ecology. He is co-author of *Time*, a volume in the LIFE Library of Science, and is author of *Climate, Man and History* and *On Every Side the Sea*.

The Cover: Wearing antler headdresses and caribou skins to disguise themselves, two hunters pause in their pursuit of the herd of caribou visible in the distance. Anthropologists believe that in expanding their hunting range, wanderers from Asia crossed the Bering Land Bridge between Siberia and Alaska during the height of the ice age and entered North America, perhaps more than 25,000 years ago.

The cover scene, as well as those on pages 23-33, has been re-created by superimposing paintings of early men by Burt Silverman on photographs of landscapes similar to those the first Americans might have seen as they crossed from Asia to North America over the land bridge.

ISBN 7054 0054 9

Contents

Introduction

The first Europeans to reach the Western Hemisphere in the 15th Century encountered a rich and diverse world—but a world already inhabited for thousands of years. The Europeans were completely unprepared for the people they found. They failed to understand cultures that seemed so exotic and different from their own, and they saw the Indians as savages, to be made over in their own image as quickly as possible.

In their zeal to conquer the land, the Europeans completely overlooked the roots that anchored the Indians to a fascinating and ancient past. Here were people free of almost all outside influences. The Americas, like the island continent of Australia, had existed for centuries without any real contact with the rest of the world. But unlike Australia, the New World was a place where advanced cultures had evolved, plants had been domesticated, and trade and cities had grown up.

Consider some of the achievements of the First Americans in North America alone. They crossed from Siberia as bands of nomadic hunters in pursuit of beasts now long vanished from the land: giant bison and mammoths. Thousands of years later their descendants were farming the arid Southwest and building the multistory apartment houses called pueblos. Meanwhile, in the river valleys of the South-east, other ancient North Americans were establishing the centres of large and complex city-states based on flourishing trade and agriculture. And the native peoples of the Northwest Pacific Coast were exploiting nature's bounty so effectively that, without the support of agriculture, they developed a brilliant culture and amassed quantities of wealth.

Obviously, the world would have been a different place had the original Americans reversed the order of things and conquered the Old World, spreading native American culture to the far corners of the earth. But since they did not, all that has survived of their magnificent prehistoric past is our knowledge of it. The importance of this past is often overlooked. History books generally begin the story of America from the first European settlement and give scant attention to the 30,000 years of separate cultural development. This book tells us of this development as it took place on the North American continent. It is an exciting story that must be pieced together from the frail clues of archaeology, since there are no written records. But the search for prehistoric America, from Alaska's frozen tundra to the sun-baked banks of the lower river Mississippi, has revealed an array of diverse cultures, growing, interacting and achieving sometimes spectacular climaxes through the centuries.

James Deetz
Brown University

Chapter One: Settlers of the New World

An American Indian, listening to an argument among white men over whether Christopher Columbus or Leif Ericson was the true discoverer of America, is said to have exclaimed: "Discover, nothing! *We* knew it was here all the time!" There is, of course, not the slightest doubt that the first men to reach the New World were neither Norse nor Genoese but the members of some nameless band of primitives, the ancestor's of today's Indians. But how and when they got to America is one of the most intriguing and most debated puzzles in prehistory—and one whose solution is only now emerging. Having arrived, they proceeded to develop a dizzying diversity of cultures, including such incredibly rich and complex societies as the mysterious Mound Builders of the Midwest, whose achievements are just beginning to be appreciated. No rude hunters, they lived in big urban centres supported by intensively cultivated farms, built huge monuments and prospered as efficient businessmen, operating factories, pottery works and an export-import trade over several thousand miles of land and water routes.

In the process of spawning this near-civilization, the ancient Indians had to take over an enormous but untouched land mass and learn to thrive in an extraordinary variety of habitats. Considering only America north of present-day Mexico (the area with which this book is concerned), man's new home included near-tropical desert in the Southwest, the rich and rainy forests and fjords of the Northwest Coast, the illimitable grasslands of the plains, woodlands ranging from subarctic to subtropical and even bleak tundra along the polar seas.

To be sure, by the time the New World was occupied, Old World man had been adapting to new habitats and ecosystems for something like a million years—ever since he first moved out of his tropical birthplace to become a wanderer on the face of the earth. But these European and Asian explorers were primitive creatures, whose early ecological adjustments moved at a glacially slow pace and have left only the most exiguous traces. The settlers of the New World, by contrast, were from all the evidence men like ourselves, *Homo sapiens sapiens* of the type called Cro-Magnon, and their spread into their immense habitat, compared with earlier population movements, progressed at the speeded-up pace of an old movie. And while the first stages of the process are still dim, reconstruction of them is enormously aided by the fact that the final stages were seen and recorded in some detail by literate, if not always accurate, observers. In Europe and (with only a few exceptions) Asia, Stone Age man lived and died with no witnesses; in the New World, he was known to some of our great-great-grandfathers.

Speculation about the original discoverers of America began almost as soon as it became apparent that the aborigines were not, as Columbus had thought, natives of the East Indies—though the misnomer that derives from his misapprehension has clung to them ever since. Momentarily, indeed, they were classed as perhaps not really human; they were not, after all, mentioned in the Bible. By 1512, how-

A proud descendant of North America's first settlers, this Nebraska Sioux, photographed in 1907, displays the straight hair, dark eyes and lack of beard that mark him clearly as an Indian. Despite physical similarities Indians shared, they became an extremely diverse people. Adapting over thousands of years to the continent's many environments, they developed widely different cultures and over 200 languages bearing no resemblance to those of their Asian ancestors.

ever, the Pope declared officially that the New World's "Indians" were true descendants of Adam and Eve. As such, they must obviously have come from the Old World's Garden of Eden.

One of the earliest and most persistent theories about the origin of the Indians—a few people still believe it—identified them as descendants of the Biblical "Lost Tribes of Israel" who had somehow made their way to the New World. This notion was held by, among others, William Penn and the New England theologian Cotton Mather—the latter proclaiming that the Indians had not migrated to America but had been brought here by the devil. Other writers linked them to an incredible variety of peoples, both real and mythical, including the Greeks, Trojans, Phoenicians, Romans, Egyptians, Ethiopians, French, English, Welsh, Danes and the inhabitants of the lost continents of Atlantis and Mu.

Curiously, however, less fanciful commentators had almost from the beginning put together clues to the correct answer. In 1950 a Spanish Jesuit, José de Acosta, wrote (as translated by a contemporary): "It is not likely that there was another Noes Arke, by the which men might be transported into the Indies, and much lesse any Angell to carie the first men to this new world, holding him by the haire of the head, like to the Prophet Abacuc. . . . I conclude, then, that it is likely the first that came to the Indies was by shipwracke and tempest of wether." De Acosta, however, realized that "shipwracke" would hardly explain how animals had arrived in America. He decided that somewhere to the north there must exist a part of America joined to the Old World, or at least "not altogether severed and disjoined, over which the animals had walked." This was nearly a

century and a half before Vitus Bering sailed through the strait that now bears his name, where America and Asia are indeed "disjoined" by less than 60 miles of water (in clear weather both continents can be seen from the centre of the strait).

A generation after De Acosta, Edward Brerewood, an Englishman, attempted to pinpoint the Indians' place of origin, and considering the sketchy information he had to go on, he did well. Because of their colour, he concluded, the Indians "are not of the Africans progeny". Furthermore, "they have no rellish nor resemblance at all, of the Artes, or learning, or civility of Europe," nor, for that matter, of China, India or other civilized parts of Asia. What was left was the "Tartars"—a rather vague term referring to the inhabitants of central and northeast Asia—to whose "rude" and "barbarous" culture Brerewood found American parallels. Like De Acosta, he postulated a land connection, or near-connection, between the Old World and the New, and placed it precisely where Bering would later find it: in "that Northeast part of Asia possessed by the Tartars".

Brerewood erred in equating Indian and "Tartar" cultures. They have few similarities. But his conclusion, arrived at for the wrong reasons, was correct. The Indians were more like the inhabitants of Asia than of any other region. Some two centuries later, the great naturalist Alexander von Humboldt pointed to the true similarities—physical features—when he noted a "striking analogy between the Americans and the Mongol race," meaning those peoples of eastern Asia whom anthropologists now term Mongoloids. Modern physical anthropology has confirmed Von Humboldt's analogies. While it is by no means true that, as earlier travellers often put it, "he who has seen one tribe of Indians has seen all," they are considerably more alike than the inhabitants of, say, Europe or Africa—and most of the traits they have in common are also found among the Mongoloid peoples all the way from Siberia to Indonesia.

In colour, Indians are "medium"—meaning that both white and dark brown to black tints are missing: they range from a dusky yellowish white to a light milk chocolate, with the majority bronze or coppery. Their eyes are dark brown; their hair is black, coarse and straight, thick on the head (baldness is rare) but sparse on the rest of the body. Their cheekbones are almost invariably wide, giving the eyes a somewhat elongated look. Perhaps the most striking similarity between Indians and East Asians is a curious trait called shovel incisor, in which the inner surfaces of the upper front teeth are concave, as though scooped out. Among both Indians and East Asians the incidence of this trait is 90 per cent or more; among other peoples, 15 per cent or less. There are other, more recondite resemblances, but the point hardly needs belabouring: no scientist today doubts that American Indians are genetically most akin to the present peoples of East Asia.

But if the Indians are clearly related to the Asian Mongoloids, they are equally clearly not identical with them. The most obvious difference, in fact, is as plain as the nose on Sitting Bull's face: the Indians' characteristic "hawk" nose. Although by no means universal among Indians, it is fairly common; by contrast, it is virtually unknown among East Asians, most of whom have conspicuously flat profiles. Further, while the Indians' eyes are often narrowed, they are almost never surrounded by the fleshy eyelids and eyelid folds that give East Asian eyes their characteristic slanted appearance. The Indians, in short, must represent a distinctive and independent branch of Asian stock, one that migrated from Siberia at a time when the modern East Asians had not yet evolved many of their special characteristics.

Much more closely related to the East Asians are those other native Americans—the Eskimos and their relatives, the Aleuts of the Alaskan islands. Many, if appropriately dressed, could not be picked out of a crowd in Peking or Tokyo. Their close resemblance to modern Mongoloids indicates that the Eskimos and Aleuts are much more recent migrants to America than the Indians. Confirming this physical link are affinities between the Eskimo-Aleut languages and such still-spoken northeast Asian tongues as Kamchadal and Chukchi; no such relationships can be demonstrated for American Indian tongues.

If most anthropologists now agree that the first Americans came from northeast Asia and entered the New World in the general area of the Bering Strait, they have long disagreed—and often fiercely—over how the settlers came and, especially, when they came. The answer to the first of these questions is very much tied up with the answer to the second. Estimates of man's age in the New World have been almost as diverse, and sometimes quite as fantastic, as the early theories of his racial or cultural relationships. A 19th Century Argentine professor turned up a skull that he claimed was one million years old —proving, he said, that Homo sapiens had actually originated in America (in Argentina, naturally). This and other notions, only somewhat less dubious, aroused a 20th Century backlash, which led to the opinion that New World man was a relative newcomer. The brief tenure of men in America formed the majority view of America's leading anthropologists, including the most influential of all, Aleš Hrdlička of the Smithsonian Institution.

Hrdlička rightly insisted that speculation about man's migration to America be grounded on solid evidence—fossil bones and tools whose ages could be generally agreed on—and all the evidence had convinced him that man had not arrived in the New World until well after the end of the last ice age, when the great ice sheets that once blanketed much of North America had disappeared and many of the animals contemporary with them had become extinct. Anybody proposing a preglacial or even an early postglacial arrival of man could expect a strong denunciation from Hrdlička. Thus before the mid-1920s few archaeologists were willing to risk their careers by suggesting, at least in public, that America had been settled more than a few thousand years prior to the Christian Era. The first arrivals, then, must have crossed the 56 miles of the Bering Strait by boat, a reasonable supposition since maritime people elsewhere in the world used boats by that time.

The discovery that began breaking down this official view traces back to a new chance find made not by an archaeologist but by a black New Mexico cowboy. One day in 1908—according to the most likely of several versions of the story—George McJunkin was riding along the edge of an arroyo that recently had been gouged deeper by flood waters. Glancing across at the opposite bank, his eye was caught by some bleached bones exposed by the flood and lying about 10 feet below the arroyo's rim. Fortunately for science, McJunkin was not only sharp-eyed but curious. He was, of course, familiar with cattle bones, but 10 feet

Three fossil bones from a bison, and the flint spear point (bottom left) that killed it, shown here still embedded in the clay in which they were found near Folsom, New Mexico, upset the belief that man was a recent arrival in America. The bison was a type extinct some 10,000 years, proving a human spear wielder was present that long ago.

below the surface of the ground seemed an odd place for them to be. Scrambling down into the arroyo he dug out some of the bones with a pair of barbed-wire clippers and took them back to the ranch.

McJunkin puzzled over his findings, which were much more massive than any cattle bones he had ever seen, and chatted about them with neighbours in and about Folsom. Over the next 18 years other amateur diggers visited McJunkin's "Bone Pit", and finally in 1926 a sampling of the strange bones was taken for identification, to palaeontologist Jesse D. Figgins, Director of the Colorado Museum of Natural History. As McJunkin had known, they were indeed not cow bones. They were bison bones—and not those of the modern bison either, but of an extinct, larger relative with horns like a Texas longhorn, that had vanished with the glaciers some 10,000 years ago.

That same year Figgins arranged for the museum to begin excavation at the "Bone Pit". Soon the site had yielded not only fossil bones but a stone point that seemed to be associated with them. Its shape was strikingly different from that of other arrowheads found nearby. The edges were almost parallel instead of tapered, the base had been chipped into a concave curve, and both sides were grooved.

But man-made flint points mixed in with the bones of ice-age bison? By the official theory this conjunction was impossible. So when word reached the Colorado Museum in 1927 that a similar flint point had turned up clearly embedded in the earth between two bison ribs, Figgins—who was keenly interested in the problem of man's antiquity in the New World —was unable to curb his excitement. He decided to go to Folsom and see for himself. He went and he saw —but a great deal of careful work was required

before his sceptical colleagues could be convinced of the association between the stones and bones. Figgins eventually had to invite some of his more severe critics to visit the Folsom site and actually examine a flint point lying between a pair of bison ribs.

Their observations ultimately led to something quite rare in archaeological circles; virtually unanimous agreement that the find meant what it seemed to mean. The discovery of the Folsom bison hunters established man's arrival in the New World in the ice age. Then, in 1932, another New Mexico site near Clovis yielded the bones of extinct animals accompanied by stone points that differed from the Folsom type. But these were discovered beneath layers of earth containing Folsom points—thus pushing man's New World tenancy as far back as 12,000 years ago.

These findings focused attention anew on the related question of how man had reached the New World. For if, as now seemed unarguable, he had travelled as far south as New Mexico during the latter part of the ice age, he must have left Siberia at least a few thousand years earlier. At that time he need not have paddled over to North America by boat, as the late-arriving Eskimos and Aleuts probably did, nor crossed 50-odd miles of tumbled, hazardous pack ice that even today occasionally fills the Bering Strait. He could have walked across on dry land.

A land bridge existed then between Asia and Alaska. It had appeared when the glaciers of the last ice age were at their peak, locking up in ice millions of cubic miles of precipitation that would normally have gone into the oceans. The absence of this water lowered the level of the Bering Sea more than 300 feet, enough to turn the shallows of the Bering Strait into a bridge of land connecting the two continents. Bridge is hardly the right word, suggesting as it does a narrow isthmus. Beringia, as this now-submerged land is called by geologists, was at its greatest extent a thousand miles or so across, making it perhaps the widest bridge on record.

Ice-age animal migrations across Beringia shaped much of the present and recently extinct animal life of North America and Eurasia; the immigrants from Siberia included the bison, moose, mammoth, caribou and musk ox, most of which were to die out after the ice ages. Migrants in the reverse direction—from America into Asia—included foxes and woodchucks and, earlier, the ancestors of the modern horse, camel and wolf. If the earliest Americans were big-game hunters, as the Folsom and Clovis finds indicate, what more natural than that they should follow the game from Asia to America?

At the time the Folsom and Clovis discoveries established that men had come to the New World over a land bridge, there was no dependable method of telling when they made the trip, since dating methods were rather crude. This question was settled in the late 1940s, with the development of the carbon-14 method for telling the age of finds by measuring the content of certain radioactive carbon atoms. Carbon-14 tests showed that Folsom culture began nearly 11,000 years ago and Clovis a thousand years or so earlier. To reach mid-continent by that time, men must have crossed to Alaska no later than about 15,000 years ago—about the time that last ice age was ending and the land bridge was being submerged.

This rather neat solution to the old mystery of the Indians' ancestors soon came to seem only half a solution, however. New discoveries and reassessments of old ones kept pushing the date of man's arrival in

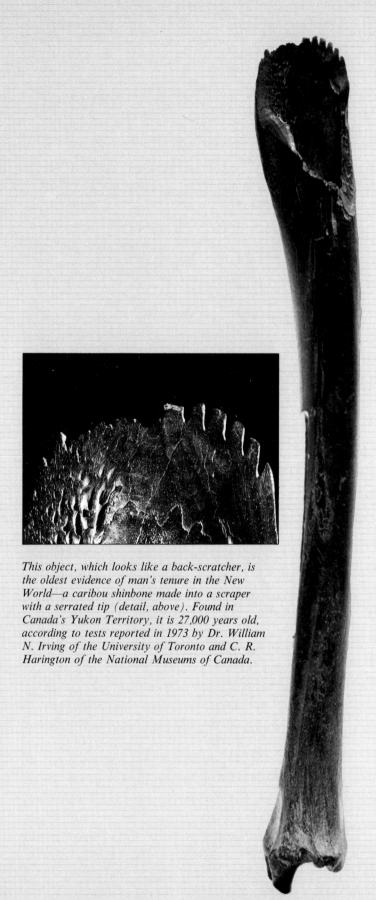

This object, which looks like a back-scratcher, is the oldest evidence of man's tenure in the New World—a caribou shinbone made into a scraper with a serrated tip (detail, above). Found in Canada's Yukon Territory, it is 27,000 years old, according to tests reported in 1973 by Dr. William N. Irving of the University of Toronto and C. R. Harington of the National Museums of Canada.

America further back in time. And every change in date raised new questions about how he came.

Among the bits of evidence that had to be explained were the bones of dwarf mammoths found on Santa Rosa Island off southern California. The bones were split and burned as though at a man-made hearth, and carbon-14 dating set their age at as much as 29,000 years. There were also artifacts and mammoth bones at Valsequillo in central Mexico that dated from 20,000 years ago, and charcoal from a possible campsite near La Jolla, California, that seemed only a little younger. And from Canada's Yukon Territory, at the head of a major corridor through the glaciers that covered North America during the ice ages, came a 10-inch-long caribou-bone scraper that in 1972 was given a radiocarbon date of 27,000 years, suggesting that man was in the Far North—and heading south—at least that long ago.

Conservative archaeologists were at pains to point out that none of these dates was unequivocal. The bones on Santa Rosa could have been charred by wildfire, and the presence of datable charcoal and bone with man-made artifacts did not necessarily mean that they were linked by anything but coincidence. The caribou scraper had been found where it was washed out of a river bank; because it no longer lay in its original bed, the 27,000-year-old age given it could not be checked against the geological evidence. There was even the possibility that the bone might be as old as it appeared, but that an Indian had picked it up thousands of years later and made it into a scraper. Such arguments were valid. And yet, to a growing number of archaeologists, all these bits of evidence, although not individually conclusive, seemed to add up to a case for man's arrival in the New World more than 25,000 years ago—enough of a case, at least, to leave the door half open.

But the most exciting evidence is the cranium of a human skull found near Los Angeles in 1936 and dated in 1971. At the time of the skull's discovery, carbon-14 dating was unknown—even after it was known the test required so much bone that the cranium would have been virtually destroyed. Thus the skull went undated until the development in the late 1960s of a process needing only a small amount of bone, and based on analysis of components in bone protein. Applied to the skull in 1971, it indicated that Los Angeles man was at least 23,600 years old.

Many experts are troubled by such dating of the Los Angeles skull. Its bizarre history—particularly its long museum storage—raises questions that have limited acceptance of the skull's value in establishing the story of man in America.

Scholars are even more wary of a 1974 report based on a test of other California bones by a different dating method. The results suggest that man may have reached the Pacific coast as much as 48,000 years ago, a date that—if accepted as accurate after much more research—would overturn many current theories about the first Americans, and raise thorny new questions about who they were and how they arrived in the Western Hemisphere.

If the Los Angeles skull is indeed as old as the protein analysis indicates, men must have been living in America for at least 25,000 years. And this possibility imposed a strange and complicated schedule on their migration to the New World. For one thing, it narrowed the period during which they could have arrived, since there are strong reasons for ruling out an arrival time much before about 40,000 years ago.

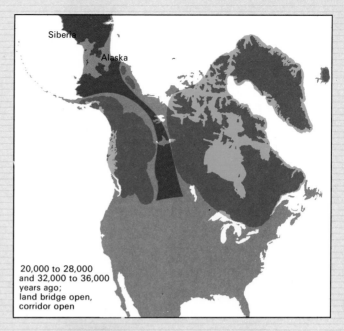

20,000 to 28,000
and 32,000 to 36,000
years ago;
land bridge open,
corridor open

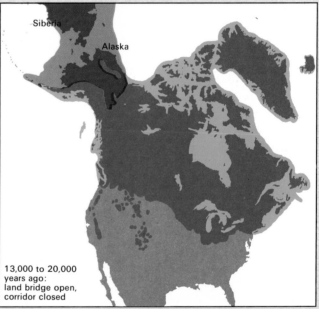

13,000 to 20,000
years ago:
land bridge open,
corridor closed

For one thing, that period marks the emergence of modern men, and all the human fossils found in the New World are of modern type. In addition, the trip to the New World by an arctic route required skills that only modern men possess. Earlier men knew how to make fires, use fur clothing and construct warm shelters—Neanderthals employed such crafts to survive in fairly cold parts of Europe during early ice ages. But not even Neanderthals had refined their skills sufficiently to survive the bitter, prolonged winters of the Far North, and apparently humans did not spread into the demanding environments that could take them to America until after the Neanderthals were replaced by modern types.

But if the first men had to come to America between 25,000 and 40,000 years ago, they had to observe a timetable set by the coming and going of glaciers during the ice age—almost like a commuter who has to catch a 7:30 bus from his street to the railway station, there make a 7:45 train and finally get an 8:30 bus to reach his office by nine. The first stage of the migrants' trip was controlled by the times the land bridge was open. During the past 40,000 years, the Beringia bridge was probably above water and open to foot traffic only twice: once from about 32,000 to 36,000 years ago, and again perhaps 13,000 to about 28,000 years ago. But the bridge was only the first leg of the complicated trip to California.

The opening of the Beringia bridge was accomplished by the accumulation of the seas' waters in gigantic inland ice sheets. Thus most of the time that the bridge was open, much of North America was ice-covered. Men might cross the bridge into western Alaska but they might not be able to get past the glaciers to reach the rest of the continent.

These maps show the land bridge that connected Siberia and Alaska at least twice during the ice ages—between 32,000 and 36,000 years ago, and between 13,000 and 28,000 years ago —when so much of the world's moisture was locked up in ice that the floor of the Bering Sea lay exposed. Men could cross this bridge at any time during both periods, but only during the first period and the early part of the second could they penetrate the heart of North America by using the glacier-free corridor (top map) that stretched down between the continental ice sheets. About 20,000 years ago the glaciers expanded so much that the land bridge widened to its maximum extent and the corridor closed (bottom map). Although men could still cross to Alaska, they now found the way south blocked and had to wait until the corridor reopened around the end of the ice ages some 13,000 years ago.

One obvious route south, along the Pacific coast, was blocked until fairly recent times by ice and formidable terrain. The most likely corridor south from the Alaskan end of the bridge was around the coast north of the Brooks Range or up the river Yukon Valley—neither region was covered by glaciers during the last ice age—into the valley of the river Mackenzie and then southwards, along the east slope of the Rockies to the Dakotas (*maps at left*). This valley was the dividing line between the great glaciers spreading eastwards from the Pacific coastal ranges and those spreading westwards from the Laurentians. At times it provided an ice-free corridor that in some places was no more than 25 miles wide. And for about seven millennia, between 20,000 and 13,000 years ago, it was completely closed; a wall of ice as much as a mile high stretched unbroken from Pacific to Atlantic, blocking all passage south.

The combination of the corridor and bridge timetables gave the ancient travellers a tight schedule. If they were not to be locked in Alaska when the Mackenzie corridor closed, roughly 20,000 years ago, they must have crossed the Beringia bridge either before it closed 32,000 years ago, or soon after it opened again 28,000 years ago. The ancestors of Los Angeles man could have made either connection, but the earlier crossing now seems likely. Artifacts that may be crude stone scrapers and choppers found at Lewisville, Texas, and other scattered sites throughout North and South America have been dated by their surroundings as early as 25,000 to 35,000 years ago. Thus, strange as it seems, some of the very first humans to reach our own evolutionary level apparently braved the rigours of the ice age Arctic to migrate from Siberia to Alaska and wander south into the centre

of the continent—all within a few thousand years.

Any traces that may remain of the first stage of this epic trek now lie beneath the waters of the Bering Sea or are still to be discovered in northeast Siberia or Alaska. For the entry of man into the New World, as for so much of his later development in America, direct evidence is scarce or totally missing. Yet much indirect evidence—drawn from geology, meteorology, anthropology and other disciplines that offer facts about other people in other times and places—can be related to the forebears of the Indians. Such extrapolation permits the reconstruction of ancient events with some confidence that the details described, while conjectural, are reasonable. Recreations of this kind, recounting prehistoric scenes as if they were being observed today, will frequently be used in this book to convey modern scholars' best estimate of the past life of man in America.

It is possible to visualize the first group of future Americans as they begin their trip to the New World, perhaps no more than 30 to 50 of them, camped somewhere on the Siberian tundra near the northern shores of the Kamchatka Peninsula. Where their ancestors came from they do not know; they know only that for uncounted generations their people have been drifting northwards, following the wandering herds of mammoth, caribou, horse, bison and other large animals that feed on the tundra's vegetation.

That this tribe lives mainly by hunting seems certain; for the better part of the year there is little other choice. During the short summers, when the barren land bursts forth with blossoms of yellow poppy and saxifrage, they can collect vegetable foods, edible roots and such. There are eggs from the migrating birds that nest on the bay shore by the millions (as

Piecing Together the Puzzle of Indian History

Key discoveries and sites associated with the story of man's settlement of prehistoric North America are marked and identified on this map. They range from the earliest human fossil found on the continent, Los Angeles man of 21,600 B.C., to the great Indian metropolis of Cahokia, Illinois, which sprawled over six square miles, contained more than a hundred ceremonial mounds and may have had as many as 20,000 inhabitants in A.D. 1100. The map also lists finds relating to the development of distinctive life styles over many thousands of years —ranging from big-game hunting to foraging and the beginnings of agriculture north of Mexico around 3000 B.C.

Ipiutak, Alaska: Largest prehistoric Eskimo settlement, A.D. 300

Independence Fjord: Earliest Greenland settlement, 2000 B.C.

Point Barrow, Alaska: Large Eskimo tool find, A.D. 500

Cape Krusenstern, Alaska: Beachfront villages occupied since 4000 B.C.

Folsom, N. Mex.: First proof of ice-age bison hunters, 8000 B.C.

Olsen-Chubbuck site, Colo.: Site of huge bison hunt, 8200 B.C.

Danger Cave, Utah: Desert foragers' site, 8000 B.C.

Boston: Giant fish weir, 2500 B.C.

Mesa Verde, Colo.: Largest cliff dwelling, A.D. 1100

Serpent Mound, Ohio: Largest effigy mound, A.D. 200

Los Angeles man: 21,600 B.C.

Cahokia, Ill.: Largest city north of Mexico, A.D. 1100

Ventana Cave, Ariz.: Grinding stone, 9300 B.C.

Bat Cave, N. Mex.: First corn north of Mexico, 3000 B.C.

Clovis, N. Mex.: Home of ice-age mammoth hunters, 9000 B.C.

Pueblo Bonito, N. Mex.: Largest pueblo, A.D. 1100

they still will 35,000 years later) and clams and mussels can be gathered along the Siberian beaches and tidal flats. There are also fish and, during spawning season, shoals of leaping salmon. Seals come ashore to breed in their hundreds of thousands and can be clubbed to death. But for some eight months the tundra is frozen and snow-covered: the plants palatable to man are buried or dormant, the birds have flown south, the shellfish beds are locked under the shore ice and the streams are frozen over. For the better part of the year it is hunt or starve.

Life is neither rich nor easy here at the margin of the inhabited world. But as the tribe moves northwards; it learns how to survive in the Arctic. Men, women and children wear crudely tailored fur trousers and jackets year round, and in coldest weather cover their heads with fur hoods. In summer they spend much of their time in the open, enjoying almost 24 hours of sunshine, but as the autumn darkness descends they retreat to the shelter of their skin tents or semi-underground huts, warmed by smoky fires of brush or driftwood. In a good winter, meaning one in which the autumn hunting has been successful, they may spend nearly all their time indoors; with a natural deep-freeze no farther away than the outside, food storage is no problem. In a bad winter they must go forth during the brief daylight hours to seek what they can catch—ptarmigan, arctic hare, fox. In a really bad winter, some die; the oldest may walk out into the icy night to spare their fellows the burden of feeding them.

The tribe's long drift to the north has proceeded along the relatively narrow strip of Asia between the sea on the right and the mountains, many of which are ice-capped with glacier-filled valleys. Now, turning eastwards, they are unknowingly taking their last footsteps in the Old World. Before them stretches Beringia, an expanse of rolling, treeless plains broken by an occasional range of hills and spotted with innumerable small lakes. Nearly all the land is waterlogged; parts consist of a grey-brown morass carpeted with mosses and lichens. But there are also vast tracts of fairly firm land covered with short, hardy sedges and grasses. Where the grazing is so good, the animals are numerous, and not all would seem unfamiliar to an observer from the 20th Century. Besides such now-vanished species as mammoths and sabre-toothed cats, the plains abound with horses and caribou, and on the fringe of the herds lurk wolves, waiting to make their kill.

For 10 or 20 generations the people gradually multiply and spread across this new country, unaware that they are approaching an uninhabited continent (they have never seen thickly inhabited land, after all), or that they are actors in a drama of discovery.

Once in a while a hunter, seeking caribou or wild horses in the rolling hills inland, may spy in the bank beside a stream a layer of shells like those that his wife gathered back at the beach a week before. If he and his fellows are of a curious mind, they may speculate on where these shells came from. But it will not occur to them that this solid land over which they pursue their quarry once lay beneath the sea—and will one day be reclaimed by it.

Lured by game, the people drift slowly towards a far-distant range of hills that in the future will mark the west coast of Alaska. In another 10, 20 or 50 generations they reach those hills and cross them. On the land bridge behind them the waves begin to creep farther and farther inland each year until at last Be-

Three Steps in Man's Domination of the Continent

The prehistoric Americans started out as big-game hunters, turned to foraging as population expanded and large game grew scarce, and eventually became farmers in a succession of developments traced in these maps. Map 1 shows the hunters at their peak about 9000 B.C., when they had spread to all regions free of glaciers. By about 4000 B.C. (*Map 2*), Indians throughout the continent had come to rely less on big-game hunting than on gathering smaller animals, fish and plant foods. This foraging phase was superseded in some places by agriculture, shown at its maximum extent on Map 3 in about A.D. 1000. By then the Eskimos, relative newcomers from Asia, had spread across the Arctic to Greenland.

Glacial ice	Farming
Big-game hunting	Eskimo sea hunting
Foraging	

4000 B.C.

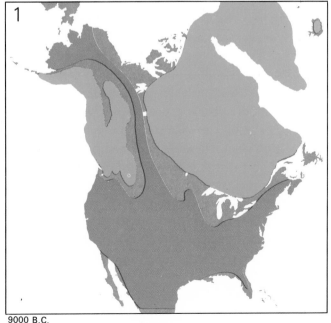

9000 B.C.

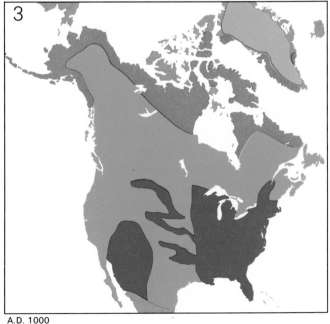

A.D. 1000

ringia is inundated by a shallow, restless sea. The people are now cut off from their past. Ahead, for some, lies another long and arduous journey into the Mackenzie watershed, the corridor between the ice sheets leading to the heartland of North America.

Once the first wanderers had trickled across to Alaska, how long did it take to occupy the rest of North and South America? Did the subsequent peopling of the continents stem from a single migration, and fairly quickly, or from successive waves of immigrants over a long period? At one time most archaeologists took the latter view. Given the extraordinary diversity of American Indian cultures, and the relatively short residence then allowed man in the New World, this was not an unreasonable conjecture: it hardly seemed possible that such cultural diversity could have developed from one group of pioneers in a mere five or six thousand years. Partly for this reason, New World man was seen as little more than a minor subsidiary of Old World man; whenever some cultural innovation turned up in America, the experts began searching for an Old World prototype.

Today, with the possibility that the first American settlers arrived no less than 25,000 years ago, and perhaps more than 30,000 years ago, the time element is no longer cogent. In 250 centuries, even people of common ancestry can develop marked cultural and physical differences. Thus, while it is possible that the Indians are the descendants of successive waves of immigrants, each introducing new ideas, it is just as possible that they spring from a relatively small number of very ancient first settlers who arrived during a fairly brief span of time. Moreover, archaeologists have now unearthed abundant evidence that many Indian cultural developments, including agriculture and the Clovis and Folsom types of stone tools, occurred independently rather than being carried over from the Old World.

Whether America was settled in one wave or several, the outcome was an extraordinary diversity of cultures. Anthropologists have catalogued thousands of different technological, artistic and social traits —all shuffled about by several thousands of years of migration, interchange and development. Most marked of the variations among Indians is language, which is a clear indicator of similarities and differences between peoples. Obviously men speaking minor variations of the same tongue—such as British and American English—are closely related, while those speaking separate yet similar languages, such as French and Italian, are more distantly related, and those using totally distinct languages, such as Chinese and German, have had no common history for a very long time. Among the Indians of North America there are more than 200 identifiable languages, some as markedly different from the others as Chinese is from German—strong evidence that their users followed independent lines of development over long periods of time.

But amidst this almost bewildering diversity there is a highly significant amount of unity. For example, the Zuñi of the Southwest spoke a language with little or no resemblance to any other Indian tongue, yet their traditional culture was much like that of many other Southwestern tribes—who themselves spoke nearly a dozen different languages. Like the Zuñi, all these tribes lived in apartment-like adobe pueblos, all practiced a simple agriculture based on corn, beans and squash, all wove blankets and made pottery that require a discerning eye to tell apart. Three tribes of what is now northern California spoke languages as different to the ear as English, Russian and Swahili—yet, as Robert F. Spencer notes in *The Native Americans*, "even a museum specialist cannot differentiate between their baskets and other tools".

This unity-amid-diversity stemmed largely from the North American Indian's dependence on the land. His capacity to modify his environment was, at best, modest. Possessing neither ox, ass nor horse, knowing neither wind power not water power, he had at his disposal only those energy resources that campfires and his own body provided. His capacity to move himself and his belongings was limited by the length of his stride and the strength of his back, or —if his journey took him over lakes, rivers or along the seashore—the capacity of his canoe and the strength of his paddling arm. If game grew sparse or his simple crops were blighted by spring frost or summer drought, he could not draw on food resources many miles distant, but had to rely on the seeds, berries, nuts and roots that could be found near by.

Because the ancient Indians were so completely dependent on the land around them, their surroundings shaped their lives. Environment determined culture more than location, chronology or even tradition. Tribes might be widely separated by time, geography and genetic relationship yet share similar cultures if the ecologies of their homelands were similar. But of course this environmental influence was affected by the gradually developing sophistication of these early Americans. In the beginning they lived primarily by hunting large mammals; following this hunting, or "Palaeo-Indian," period came a time when a greater variety of resources, both plant and animal, were exploited. In this "Foraging," or "Archaic," period, man's increasingly intensive and efficient exploitation of relatively restricted regions made possible the first semipermanent settlements. Finally, in the "Formative" period, the beginning of agriculture turned some settlements into more or less year-round villages and eventually cities—one, Cahokia in Illinois, had a population of many thousands by A.D. 1000.

Like cultural types everywhere, the three identified in North America blurred and overlapped, influenced always by environment. The foraging cultures did not simply follow the hunting cultures; in some places they existed simultaneously. Nor was either replaced everywhere: the northernmost Indians and the Eskimos remain essentially hunting peoples, while foragers persisted until well after the appearance of the white man. Finally, even where earlier stages of culture were superseded, they were never replaced totally; neither foragers nor farmers abandoned hunting completely, nor did farmers cease gathering wild plants to supplement their crops. The three stages might better be considered three life styles, differing more in emphasis than in kind.

These life styles are especially noteworthy because they worked so well for so long. After more than 25,000 years of occupancy, the Indian left the land as rich, as wild and as beautiful as his immigrant ancestors had found it. He was a resounding ecologic success. For him the primeval forest, the virgin prairie, the sun-struck desert were never out of sight, and seldom more than a few dozen steps away from his campfire. The first American was part of nature and she of him; he knew her richness and beauty, her harshness and menace, as not one modern American in 10,000 does.

How America Was Found, by Accident

In a strange way, it was the ocean floor that drew the first humans to North America. They walked from Asia on what had been ocean bottom until the ice ages exposed it as a "bridge" called Beringia. It had accumulated the natural fertilizers of sea animal and plant remains, on which grew lush forage that lured animals from Asia; the animals lured men.

The people of these times—known from archaeological finds in Siberia—were big-game hunters, although they also supplemented their diet with plants and birds. In autumn, when the herds retreated to winter refuges in Alaska, the hunters followed—eventually to become the first Americans.

Their backs to the low arctic sun, hunters leave Asia behind as they follow a caribou trail leading them east—to North America.

Setting up camp, a man drapes the hide of a bison over the framework of a pit house, while two women secure the bottom edges with roc

...nother woman roasts meat over a fire, and a fourth scrapes the skin of a freshly killed caribou.

Mobile Homes for a Trek across the Tundra

During the brief summer, bands of hunters roamed the treeless plains of Beringia in search of big game. Whenever they came to a particularly promising area, such as a caribou gathering place, they did as their ancestors had done before them in Siberia, and set up their crude pit houses, so named because they were partially sunk into the ground for protection against the cold and wind.

These houses were constructed by scraping a hollow in the ground about a foot deep and at least six feet in diameter, and then erecting over the shallow pit a frame of sticks or mammoth bones. Furs and skins draped over the frame, tied down with thongs and weighted around the bottom with stones, dirt or pieces of sod helped to seal out the wind. Furs covered all of the floor except a space in the centre for a hearth. But there was no keeping out the swarms of mosquitoes that bred in Beringia's thousands of ponds and lakes, and the hunters often were obliged to wear their hide clothing day in and day out or risk being eaten alive by the insects.

Such shelters could be taken apart quickly and easily and the supports rolled up with furs, hides and food to be hauled to the next camping ground. Only with the approach of winter did the wandering end; then the hunters settled down in some protected site, there to stock-pile supplies of meat and wait out the punishing cold.

The shimmering iridescence of the northern lights silhouettes fur-clad hunters bringing the day's catch back to their fire-lit pit houses. One hun

ries the carcass of a steppe antelope; the other has ptarmigans hanging from a stick. A small boy who is learning to hunt accompanies them.

Caribou: Staple of the Beringians

After Beringia's long, dark winter, during which temperatures remained well below zero for weeks on end and the wind blew relentlessly out of the north, no sight could have been more welcome to the hungry hunters than that of the caribou coming back to their calving grounds in spring. Strung out in long, wavering lines, these migratory animals returned from their winter shelter in the mountains of Alaska and Siberia year after year as though on schedule.

Caribou, perhaps more than any other animal, were essential to the survival of the Beringians. Numbering in the hundreds of thousands, they provided a range of products—delicious meat and fat for food, hides to turn into clothing, sinews for thread, and bones and antlers from which the hunters fashioned everything from skin scrapers to needles.

The winter coats of the returning caribou were especially desirable: soft and plushy, they made warm, comfortable garments. What the hunters could not have known is why the skins were so warm: caribou hairs, unlike those of most other animals, contain microscopic hollow spaces that block heat loss, making the fur one of nature's best insulators.

Hunters disguised as caribou plan an attack on a herd migrating through the spring snow towards

...alving grounds. The men, by creeping upwind, will be able to approach the herd unnoticed and kill some animals before the others stampede.

A Wealth of Small Game

A ptarmigan in summer plumage sits camouflaged on its nest on the ground as foragers, unaware of the bird's presence, pick seeds.

Coming upon a rookery of Steller's sea lions, hunters attack two pups that they separated from their mothers.

Beringia offered the bands that lived on it a range of foods. For those dwelling closest to the shores, there were sea lions, seals and walruses, fish and shellfish, and waterfowl of all kinds, whose eggs, in spring, must have brought welcome relief to the monotony of a meat diet. Inland, the basic fare of caribou, bison, horse and mammoth could be varied in summer with roots, greens and berries.

One morsel available year-round was the ptarmigan, a plump bird that still inhabits Alaska and changes its plumage with the seasons—in summer it is a mottled red, brown and ochre (*left*); in winter, white. In spite of its camouflage, the ptarmigan is easy to catch. Confident of its invisibility, it sits on its nest and lets predators approach, then struts off to lure them from its eggs or young. To the Beringians, this behaviour would have been a giveaway of the nest, and they could have easily scooped up the eggs or pursued the bird itself.

The First Steps into a Virgin Land

Exactly when the hunters of Beringia set foot for the first time on the soil of North America, no one will ever know—but surely there must have been a small band like this one whose members, pressing on in search of game, became, without ever knowing it, the discoverers of America.

The people's dependence on herd animals led them into the New World. Caribou, bison and horses could not survive the winter on Beringia, partly because it was so cold but mainly because snow and ice covered most of the forage. In autumn the animals migrated east and west, finding in both Siberia and Alaska sheltered valleys and forest patches where they could live until spring.

Men followed. Some bands must have left the plain of Beringia to venture into the forbidding Brooks Range of Alaska (*right*). Ruts cut in the ground by the herds would have pointed the way through the passes into the sheltered valleys—and the valleys in turn would have taken the hunters onwards, deeper and deeper into the virgin continent.

Approaching North America, a small band of hunters survey the mountains of Alaska, blue under

veak light of late summer. They will shelter in the valleys for the winter, before pushing on in the spring in search of new hunting grounds.

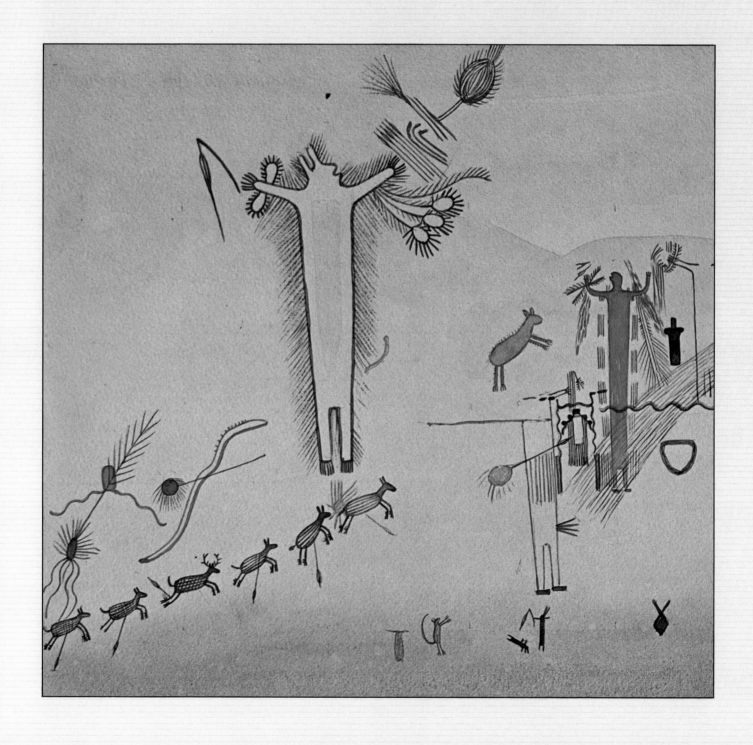

It is around 40,000 years ago, and the heart of North America has yet to feel the tread of a human foot or hear the sound of a human voice. The country is beautiful and rich, an immense, untouched sweep of undulating land stretching from the Rocky Mountains to the Mississippi and from Canada to Mexico. The climate is chilly and moist, for to the north a nearly solid topping of ice a mile thick covers most of the continent. Winds blowing off the glaciers not only cool the air but also bring to the plains enough rainfall to sustain a lush cover of vegetation in regions that will someday be semiarid or arid.

On the northern plains between what will later be Wyoming and Iowa, the lower and wetter areas are forested with pine, spruce and tamarack; the higher land, except for wooded lake margins and river valleys, is open and parklike, carpeted with grass. Further south, the limitless plains extend for hundreds of miles west of the Mississippi in a broad belt consisting partly of woodland in which birch, alder and other deciduous trees mingle with conifers, partly of prairie grasslands scattered with lakes and ponds. Beyond this belt, rolling long-grass plains interspersed with the twining fingers of river-valley forests reach to the foothills of the Rockies. On the other side of the Rockies, Nevada is covered by Lake Bonneville, as large as some of the Great Lakes of the 20th Century (Great Salt Lake will be Bonneville's

Depicted in ghostly elongated style, Indian shamans invoke the spirits of the hunt in this 1,000-year-old cave painting from the river Pecos area of Texas. The large figure, draped with pouches for hunting gear from the tough skin of the prickly pear, holds arrows or spears in one hand and an atlatl, a spear-launching device, in the other. Deer— some of them wounded—run across the bottom of the scene, straight towards the other weapon-wielding shamans.

much abridged remnant); even Death Valley sustains a sizeable body of fresh water.

The green plains are one enormous zoo—filled with some of the most remarkable animals the continent has known. In low, well-watered parts of the northern plains the giant moose *Cervalces*, its antlers towering eight feet or more overhead, browses along the marshy lake shores. In the streams, foraging for water plants, are *Castoroides*, beavers as big as modern bears with chisel-like incisors up to eight inches long. On the woodland edges ground sloths, incongruous small heads topping elephant-sized bodies, rear up on their haunches to nibble foliage 20 feet above the ground, occasionally reaching even higher with long, curved claws to pull down a leafy branch. In more open country roam herds of long-horned bison, caribou, musk oxen and shrub oxen, the last only a little larger than mountain sheep. Dwarfing all —even the huge ground sloths—are the gigantic mammoths. The largest of them, the imperial mammoth, stands 14 feet at the shoulder, tall enough to look into a second-story window, its inward-curving tusks at least twice as long as those of a 20th Century elephant. Only slightly smaller than the imperial is the woolly mammoth, whose already formidable bulk is made to seem greater by a shaggy coat of coarse, reddish hair.

In the mixed woodland and grasslands to the south, the animal life is richer still. Here, along with herds of mammoths, are their more solitary, tree-browsing cousins: the mastodons, matching the woolly mammoths in size and, like them, covered with coarse, reddish hair; and the superbison, whose horns, shaped like elephant tusks, spread six feet from tip to tip. Camels, peccaries, jack rabbits and other smaller animals are past counting, and, in season, waterfowl form a living blanket on the prairie ponds.

On all these plant eaters, large and small, preys a fearsome array of carnivores. The dire wolf, nearly half again as large as the later timber wolf, is armed with powerful, bone-crunching jaws. The bobtailed sabre-toothed cat clutches its victim with massive forelimbs and stabs it to death with eight-inch-long upper canines, and a panther larger than the biggest modern lion is one of the largest predatory land animals of this or any other age.

Conspicuously missing, however, is the most efficient predator of all, man.

Far to the north, beyond the ice wall of the glaciers, there are humans. At this time, some 35,000 to 40,000 years ago, they have been entering Alaska from Asia, drifting across the intercontinental land bridge that has been exposed as more and more of the earth's water has accumulated in glaciers, reducing ocean levels. Game has lured these men to the New World, and they are expert hunters. They have to be, for in all their ancestral homeland in Siberia, as well as in Alaska, hunting is the only way to survive. The climate is too cold to produce a year-round supply of plant food, but there is always plenty of meat on the hoof.

If the pursuit of game has drawn the first men to subarctic America, there is little doubt that the promise of even better hunting is what is leading them to press south towards the Great Plains.

Every autumn, huddled on the snowy tundra near the Arctic Circle, they see the sun dip lower and lower on the horizon. They watch as daylight dwindles until, for the greater part of their waking hours, their only outdoor light is the glitter of the polar stars, the pale luminescence of the Northern Lights or the cold brilliance of the moon. And as the days visibly shorten, they see the skeins of swans, geese and ducks, the clouds of curlews, plovers and sandpipers fly southwards from arctic breeding grounds. The birds are followed in turn by the horses, bison, caribou and mammoths. Meanwhile, the snows drift ever deeper, and even small game is less often seen. Given these conditions, it requires no great imagination to deduce that by following the vanishing sun, as did the birds and beasts, one can find more game.

In this press to the south, both migrating herds and the men who prey on them must bypass the formidable glaciers that almost wall Alaska. Some wander along the bleak arctic coast north of the Brooks Range, and others follow the rugged course of the river Yukon; those are the two routes into the valley of the Mackenzie. This valley has yet to ice over completely, and for a few thousand years one small band of immigrants after another can drift between its limestone slopes with their covering of sedges and dwarf trees. As the travellers approach what will someday be the province of Alberta, they may confront the life-destroying glaciers at closer range, narrowing the open corridor to perhaps 25 miles. But a few hundred miles to the southeast the glacial ice once again recedes from view, and opening before them they find the seemingly infinite expanse of the plains country, the land of the big sky that never fails to amaze those who see it for the first time.

Of these first pioneers of the American West, only a few traces can now be found. Stones that look as though they had been used as tools by man, found in New Mexico and Texas among other places, plus the skull of Los Angeles man, given a date of 23,600 years, suggest that humans had made the trip south from Alaska. But such finds tell little about how they lived during these ancient days.

In hunting practices, and most living habits, the very early Americans had little reason to change from the ways of their northern forebears. But in one respect their new home on the plains was radically different from their ancestral lands of the north, and this difference could not help but affect their life style. Whereas the north was almost devoid of plant foods, the plains were rich in vegetation. There must have been occasions, once the game learned to fear man, when meat was less easy to come by or when simple dietary curiosity prompted the hunters to try other fare. At such times the plant resources of the plains—edible roots, nuts, wild berries or fruits —probably did not go unappreciated. For energy there were starchy roots of the Indian turnip, groundnut and, in marshy areas, arrowhead, as well as the ground bean, which could be found in the underground caches of the prairie vole. For really hard times, there would have been the roots of the bush morning-glory, which, though not very palatable, are both enormous and nutritious. For variety there would have been wild currants, gooseberries, serviceberries and high-bush cranberries, while the more southerly areas yielded buffalo berries, chokecherries, wild plums, papaws and persimmons, plus nuts of the hazel, pecan, black walnut and hickory.

Amid such plenty, the early Americans prospered and spread over the continent. There is evidence —mostly rough stone tools whose significance is still uncertain—of their presence from California to Colorado, Oregon and Arizona. Even in South America

stone artifacts perhaps 20,000 years old have been found. A journey that far south must have involved a lengthy sojourn in the dense forests covering most of Central America. It is possible that climatic changes resulting from the advance of the ice sheets farther north may have thinned these jungles somewhat, but even so, the journey argues for considerable ingenuity in adapting to radically different terrain, plants and animals. Thus it is not inconceivable that other groups of ingenious and perhaps restless plainsmen reached the forest-covered shores of the Atlantic.

But for all their apparent achievements, these early Americans remain shadowy figures. The first unambiguous and even moderately abundant evidence of the lives of ancestral Indians comes from a time nearly a thousand generations after the first arrivals —between 11,000 and 12,000 years ago. The setting is still the plains—specifically that portion spreading across eastern New Mexico and western Texas and known to early Spanish explorers as the Llano Estacado, or Staked Plains. The glaciers have passed their peak and have been retreating for some millennia. The climate, however, remains much the same as the first men had found it, cool and fairly moist, and the Llano Estacado—semiarid in the 20th Century—is, during this earlier period, an expanse of green, tree-sprinkled grassland dotted with little ponds and seamed with wooded river valleys. The animal life continues to be abundant and diverse.

The only striking difference is in the men who hunt the animals. They are the people known for their skilfully made fluted stone weapons, the Clovis spear points (page 42). Being hunters, they rove most of the time—small, family-sized bands of them going

An American Zoo: Animals Man Found

When ancient man spread into North America some 25,000 years ago, he found a continent alive with game —many, like himself, immigrants. The chart below shows 57 of the more important mammals he discovered.

In the block on the left are animals, including man, that walked from Asia to North America across the Bering Land Bridge connecting the two continents at various times over eight million years; the block at right shows those that originally came from South America, and the one in the centre those that evolved in North America. The arrows indicate the directions the animals followed in their movements into and out of North America; some,

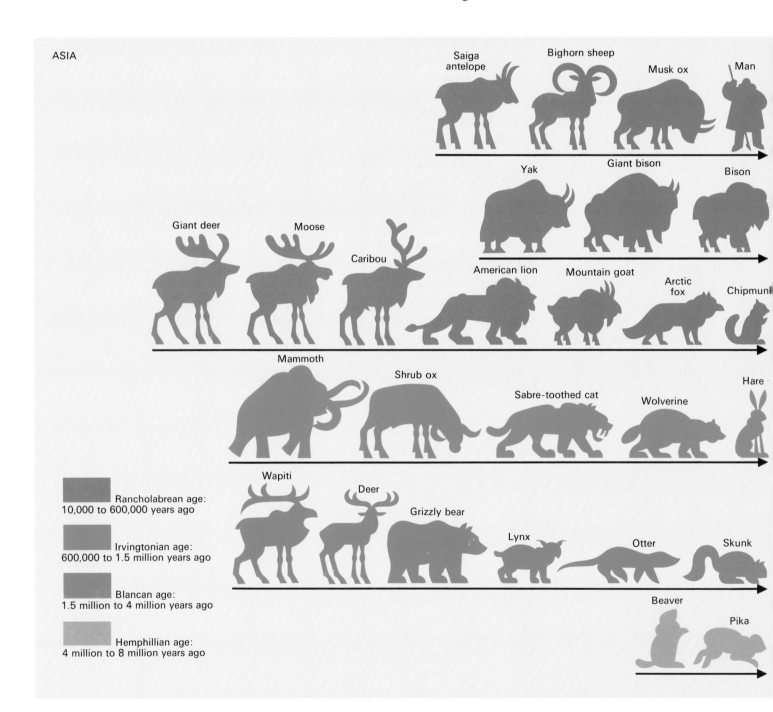

ASIA

Saiga antelope Bighorn sheep Musk ox Man

Yak Giant bison Bison

Giant deer Moose Caribou American lion Mountain goat Arctic fox Chipmunk

Mammoth Shrub ox Sabre-toothed cat Wolverine Hare

Wapiti Deer Grizzly bear Lynx Otter Skunk

Beaver Pika

Rancholabrean age:
10,000 to 600,000 years ago

Irvingtonian age:
600,000 to 1.5 million years ago

Blancan age:
1.5 million to 4 million years ago

Hemphillian age:
4 million to 8 million years ago

like the mammoth and bison, arrived from Asia, while others, like the wolf and fox, arose in the New World and eventually spread to Asia.

The bright colours indicate the time period when each animal began its migration. These times are keyed below to North American mammalian ages —Hemphillian, Blancan, Irvingtonian and Rancholabrean—according to a dating system named after fossil sites. For example, between 600,000 and 1.5 million years ago, in the Irvingtonian age, the modern horse came to North America from Asia, eventually to die out here and not appear again until it was reintroduced by the Spaniards in historic times. Animals that evolved in North America and never left it are shown in grey; their position indicates the age when they evolved into the forms depicted. Thus the pronghorn antelope, a product of the Rancholabrean age, 10,000 to 600,000 years ago, stands between animals that are coloured purple to denote their migration during this age.

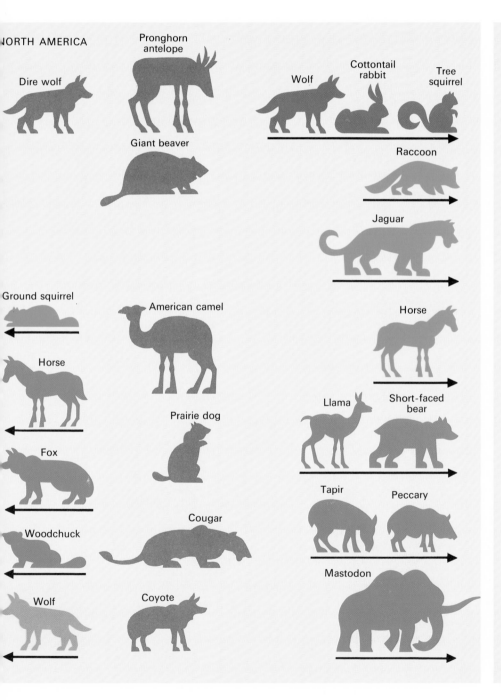

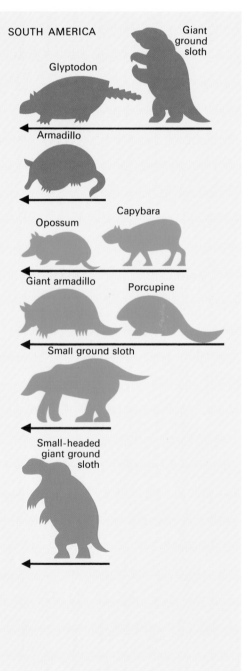

from one temporary camp to another, wherever the game leads. In areas where prey is especially plentiful and the hunting continuously good, a few of their sites are occupied jointly by several bands as more or less permanent bases. But even the larger camps seem to consist of no more than rude windbreaks made of brush or grass.

However much their life style may resemble that of their ancestors, these plainsmen have one enormous advantage—the keen stone spear points that are the hallmark of their culture. The seemingly delicate Clovis points are actually lethal tools, and the Clovis people make effective use of them in killing the great woolly mammoth.

Archaeologists have found ample evidence of the Clovis points' deadliness embedded in the remains of the hunters' mammoth prey. The points are typically about four or five inches long and almost perfectly symmetrical. In shape they resemble the upper third of a bayonet, the sides parallel, or nearly so, at the base and then curving in to a sharp point. The faces are carefully thinned out to improve their penetrating power, but the sharp edges are blunted near the base of the points to prevent them from cutting through the lashings that held them in the split ends of their shafts. Possibly to provide for a firmer grip on the points, the concave bases are further thinned by painstakingly detaching flakes from both faces, producing flutes that extend over one third to one half the length of the points.

The points are generally called projectile points, but whether the tools or weapons of which they formed the cutting tip were in fact projectiles is a matter of conjecture. Unquestionably they are spear points of some sort (they are far too big for arrowheads and, besides, the bow and arrow was unknown to Clovis hunters), but there is no direct evidence to show whether the spears were used primarily for thrusting, as lances, or for throwing, as javelins. Unlikely as it seems, even the immense mammoths could have been taken by men on foot, armed only with lances. This is the way elephants were hunted in Africa until quite recently. Like the modern elephant hunters, the mammoth's attackers may have worked in two groups, some acting to divert the animal's attention while others dashed in to stab at its belly and legs from close quarters.

But many experts think Clovis men avoided such dangerously close encounters by throwing their weapons at their prey. To do so effectively they would have needed an extra tool, the simple but revolutionary spear thrower, or atlatl, which enables a man to hurl his weapon from a relatively safe distance, yet with enough force to penetrate the tough hide of a mammoth. The atlatl consists of a stout stick or length of bone perhaps two feet long, one end of which is shaped into a turned-up hook. In use, the spear is laid along the stick so that the hook engages the spear butt; the hunter, grasping the other end of the stick, uses it as an extension of his arm to hurl the spear with a marked increase in speed, range and striking power. The atlatl's advantage comes from the extra length it gives a man's arm. By placing the spear farther away from the shoulder pivot, it makes the propelling swing take a wider arc, and provides higher speed. One writer has compared an atlatl-wielding spearman to a baseball pitcher whose throwing arm hangs down to his knees.

Whether these men possessed the spear thrower is

The Atlatl: A Deadly Missile Launcher

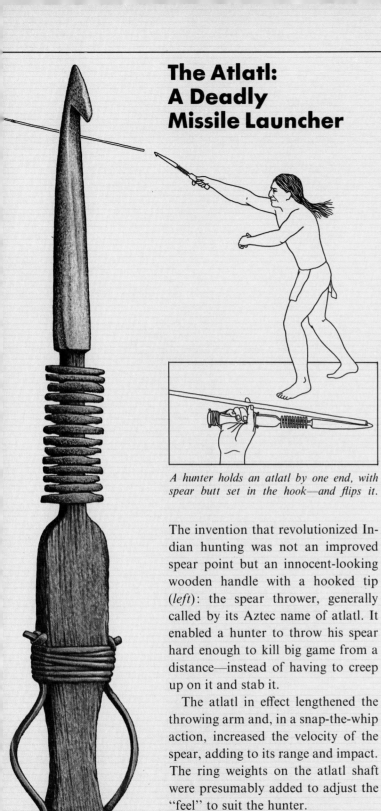

A hunter holds an atlatl by one end, with spear butt set in the hook—and flips it.

The invention that revolutionized Indian hunting was not an improved spear point but an innocent-looking wooden handle with a hooked tip (*left*): the spear thrower, generally called by its Aztec name of atlatl. It enabled a hunter to throw his spear hard enough to kill big game from a distance—instead of having to creep up on it and stab it.

The atlatl in effect lengthened the throwing arm and, in a snap-the-whip action, increased the velocity of the spear, adding to its range and impact. The ring weights on the atlatl shaft were presumably added to adjust the "feel" to suit the hunter.

Whether the Indians invented the atlatl themselves or acquired it from Asia is unknown, but it was used by them more than 10,000 years ago.

speculative, but archaeological clues suggest that the Clovis people did indeed have ways of minimizing the risks of mammoth hunting. First, virtually all their known kill sites are at locations where the nature of the soil points to the former presence of a pond or stream. The hunters could have lain in wait at such places in full confidence that the animals would eventually visit them to drink; a modern elephant requires up to 50 gallons of water a day, and a mammoth must have needed even more.

In several cases, moreover, there are indications that the hunters attacked animals that had bogged down in the marshy edges of a lake. Finds at one Clovis kill site bear a striking resemblance to those unearthed at Torralba, Spain, where 300,000 years ago Homo erectus elephant hunters had also used this technique effectively. At Torralba one of the extinct straight-tusked elephants killed in a swamp had fallen on its side. Only the exposed side had been hacked off by the hunters and carried away; the skeleton of the bogged-down side was discovered virtually intact. At the Clovis site it was the leg bones of a mammoth that were found intact, standing upright just as they had been when the beast became mired, while the rest of the mammoth's skeleton was scattered about in a manner indicating that the hunters had cut up their kill from the top down, ignoring only the hard-to-reach legs.

Such graphic evidence makes it easy to re-create the scene, some 11,000 years in the past, of a doomed mammoth trapped in the lakeside muck and surrounded by a dozen yelling Clovis hunters. The great beast, towering above its tormentors, trumpets shrilly in rage and flails about its trunk and eight-foot-long tusks. A pair of the most daring hunters dash

An Armoury of Indian Weapons

The line-up at right shows how Indian weapons developed over 12,000 years, partly in response to changes in hunting techniques. The first two spears are tipped with points called Clovis and Folsom—names commemorating the locations where these artifacts were found—and belong to the era of big-game hunting. During that period hunters would close in on ponderous land mammals and thrust their spears directly into them; the points' smooth edges enabled the spears to be jerked free for a second stab.

As populations grew, regional variations appeared. On the plains hunters used slender Eden and serrated Dalton points. In the Great Lakes region, they turned to native copper as an alternative to stone, and hammered it into shape. Elsewhere, the Indians took advantage of readily available supplies of stone, such as slate, to produce points that were ground, instead of being flaked and chipped; the ground point shown here comes from the Pacific Northwest.

When the Indians turned to foraging as a way of life they developed more varied hunting techniques, and the last three types of weapon reflect this change. Some hunters stalked swift-moving animals and threw their spears instead of stabbing with them. For this reason many foragers' points, like the Eva point, were given barbs to lodge them more securely in the flesh. The use of barbs led to side-notching as a way of fixing the point more securely to the shaft. Sometime after 1000 B.C. the bow was introduced, and a variety of arrowheads resulted. The bow and arrow remained the Indians' basic weapon until the introduction of firearms by Europeans.

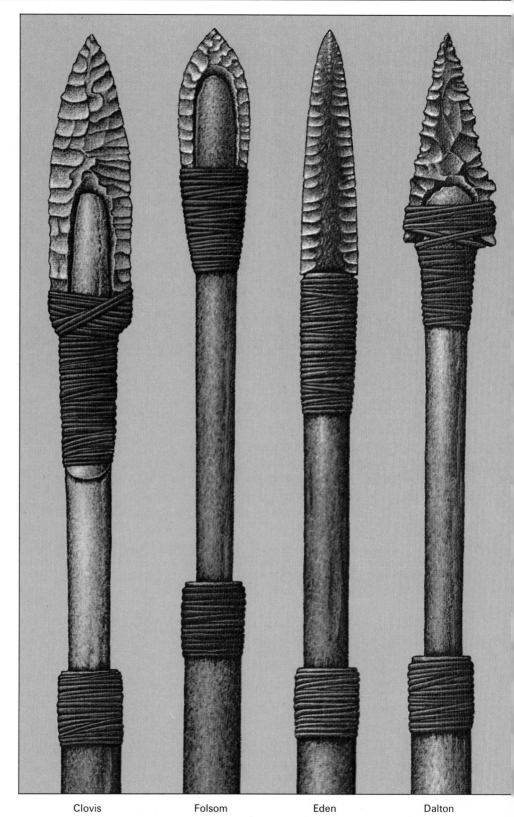

Clovis   Folsom   Eden   Dalton

Copper   Ground stone   Eva   Side-notched   Arrows

Setting the trap for the bison, an Indian hunting band closes in on a herd grazing in a field cut by dry gullies. The hunters leave open only

behind it to slash at the muscles and tendons of its hind legs. With the mammoth thus distracted, other hunters circle in front of the prey to fling their spears into its breast in hopes of piercing the lungs. At least one stone point hits home, and the wild trumpeting diminishes. As the stricken beast begins to crumple, the men close in and sink their spears deep into the soft flesh of the belly. Now certain of the feasting soon to come, the hunters retreat to solid ground to wait for the mammoth, its legs imprisoned in the blood-reddened marsh, to die.

Since mammoths, if they were anything like modern elephants, must have been intelligent beasts, they would not often have bogged down this way accidentally. It is fairly safe to assume that the hunters had worked out techniques of stampeding the animals into the treacherous lake margin. At other sites, mammoths seem to have been stampeded into a steep-sided stream gully, where they would presumably have been either injured or at least hampered in their movement. And at one place the bones uncovered are all from baby or half-grown mammoths, suggesting that the hunters had managed to cut out these less dangerous—and doubtless more tender—individuals from the herd.

Whatever Clovis man's techniques, he killed mammoths with considerable frequency; at least the bones turn up fairly consistently with his distinctively fashioned spear points. But by no means did the hunters limit themselves to mammoths: several sites also contain bones of now extinct types of horse, camel or bison. While the mammoth was undoubtedly a Large Economy Size package of food, its hide must have left a lot to be desired as material for a tent or clothing; members of the elephant family are not called pachyderms—"thick-skinned"—for noth-

An Ancient Hunt Reconstructed

During a 1950s drought, wind blowing soil from a field near Kit Carson, Colorado, laid bare vivid evidence of a prehistoric hunt—bones of extinct long-horned bison, piled in a ravine and scattered close by, mixed with stone tools and carefully chipped spear points. Archaeologists who subsequently excavated the site were able to piece together an amazingly complete picture of the hunt that occurred here 10,000 years ago. Their finds serve as the basis for the detailed drawings at left and on the following pages, showing how the Indians, long before they had the horse, preyed on the great herds of the plains.

one escape route, across a six-foot-deep ravine (foreground), into which the bison will be forced.

ing, and the hides of other large animals offered possibilities that the skins of mammoths plainly lacked. The Clovis hunters must have turned, in particular, to the bison, whose thick, shaggy coat could easily have been turned into garments warm enough to protect them from the punishing cold of the prairie winters. In time—as the artist's reconstruction of an actual bison hunt beginning on these pages indicates—the hunters learned to rely so much on this lumbering beast for hides and meat that it became the Plains Indians' principal support.

That the Clovis people themselves did work soft hides from animals like bison is more than a mere inference; several of their campsites contain sizeable numbers of stone scrapers, some of which were certainly used to remove flesh and fat from raw skins. For cutting the hides, and for butchering their prey, the Clovis hunters possessed stone knives. These im-

plements were made by striking the edge of a core of fine-grained flint or obsidian in such a way that long slivers or blades of stone flaked off—each with relatively straight edges that were as sharp as a razor.

Such a stone blade can skin an animal even faster than one of steel, as has been proved by actual test. A few years ago, a professional hunter named Gene Seeley was asked by a group of student archaeologists to shoot a destructive bear that had invaded their Arizona camp and showed no intention of leaving. Seeley killed the bear, and during a discussion of stone tools the students suggested he try to skin it with an obsidian blade. Sceptical, Seeley agreed —and then proceeded to surprise himself and his audience by skinning the entire bear, including the difficult head and paws, in less than 30 minutes, about half as long as it would have taken him to do the same job with a steel knife. The only drawback to

The leader of the hunting expedition, having given the signal to begin the attack, hurls a stone-tipped spear.

In response to the leader's signal, the hunters charge the herd, brandishing their spears, waving skins and shouting to startle the grazing animals.

the stone tool, Seeley said, was that it was almost too sharp, and he had had to take more than ordinary care to avoid slicing into the carcass itself.

What the makers of these unique tools looked like no one knows—not a single human fossil has yet been found. But of their excellent handiwork, there is abundant evidence. And it tells a story of a remarkably successful people.

Clovis-like spear points have turned up from coast to coast—at Borax Lake in central California; in the Nevada and Arizona deserts; all over the Mississippi region and northeast to Nova Scotia; as far south as Mexico and as far north as Alaska. Since no fluted points have come to light in the Old World, they appear to have been an American invention—perhaps the first—and their spread may have represented nothing more than the handing on of a new idea from

one hunting group to another. On the other hand, their continent-wide distribution could mean a movement of the Clovis people. Conceivably, the development of an especially effective hunting tool led to a population explosion among the big-game hunters and encouraged them to spread out widely from their original home—wherever that may have been—carrying their specialized spear point with them to the four corners of North America.

The spread, whether of people or only tool design, was extraordinarily rapid. The points that can be dated (many have been picked up on the surface, without a clue to their real age) all appear to fall within a span of a thousand years. And with the spread of life style based on big game into almost every part of America, there arose what seems to have been the first all-American culture—a phenomenon that would not exist again until after the European settlement

Panic-stricken, the long-horned bison close ranks, turn in the only direction left open and thunder away in a blind stampede.

some 11,000 years later. To be sure, this culture could not have been even nominally unified; distances between groups were great, and diverse habitats called for all sorts of adaptations. On the southern plains the hunters' principal prey was the mammoth, but what they hunted elsewhere is a matter of conjecture since in no other area have the Clovis-type points been found with animal bones. However, many of the distinctive points occur at sites in forested regions, and there is thus a good possibility that they were intended for killing mastodon, whose massive relics have turned up in most wooded areas of North America. In parts of Nova Scotia, which then lay only about 60 miles south of the retreating ice sheets and were almost certainly tundra-like country, the caribou seems the most plausible prey.

The hunters of 11,000 years ago must also have learned to exploit the plant resources of their varied habitats. And when they reached the shores of the Atlantic or the Pacific, they probably soon acquired a taste for shellfish and a number of other marine animals. Since any of their shoreside sites would long ago have been submerged by the rising seas as the glaciers gradually melted, the exploitation of shellfish is almost pure conjecture. But not quite.

In 1967, scientists from Woods Hole Oceanographic Institution were exploring the ocean bottom off Chesapeake Bay in the Institution's mini-submarine *Alvin.* They were studying the ice-age shoreline of the continent—and hoping to come across clues to ancient men. In the shallow, coastal zone they found a series of ocean bottom ridges, evidently remnants of dune-topped beaches such as still fringe much of the southeast Atlantic coast. And on top of one of these ridges, 140 feet below the surface of the sea, they spotted "a scattered group of oyster shells, the sort

The stampeding animals surge into the dry ravine, which is deep and broad enough to trap many of them. Falling one on top of another, they clog the ravine to become a writhing bridge over which the last of the herd escape.

Spear-wielding Indians rush up to the ravine and slaughter the bison struggling at the top of the twisted pile-up. Many of the animals underneath, crushed by the weight of bodies on top, have suffocated. In all, archaeologists counted the skulls of 193 dead bison.

of evidence that might be expected to denote the presence of early man". From what is known about postglacial changes in sea level, it seems likely that the site the *Alvin* spotted would be roughly contemporary with sites where Clovis-like points have been found and dated.

As the Clovis type of spear point was widely adopted in North America, it took on local forms. At first they differed from the prototype only slightly—some were boat-shaped, narrowing towards the base, while others were fish-shaped, narrowing and then widening. About 11,000 years ago a more radically changed design appeared—the type first discovered near Folsom, New Mexico, by the cowboy George McJunkin. Such points, differing from Clovis points most obviously in their smaller size and in fluting that extends almost the full length of the blade, are usually considered to be the hallmark of a distinctive Fol-

som people native to the southern plains. But the Folsom men were quickly replaced by—or evolved into—a group who made unfluted spear points, and are called Plano hunters by archaeologists to differentiate them from earlier men. With these new peoples came far-reaching changes in living habits.

The most striking difference between the Folsom and Plano big-game hunters and their Clovis predecessors is not in their spear points but in the types of animals they hunted. By Folsom times the mammoth had become extinct, and its place as preferred game had been taken by the American animal that from now on would be the mainstay of the Plains Indian —the bison. For thousands of years to come, the bison would provide the Indian with meat. Its tough hide—tanned with the animal's own brains—would furnish him with clothing and shelter, its dried dung would fuel his fire and its bones, horns and even its

teeth would become tools, weapons and ornaments.

The bison hunted by Folsom man was primarily *Bison antiquus*, a long-horned beast that stood six feet high at the shoulder and weighed a ton. The chief prey of the later Plano people was the somewhat smaller *Bison occidentalis* and the still smaller modern species *Bison bison*, the animal commonly called the buffalo. These creatures were far easier to kill in quantity than mammoths, since bison roamed the plains in gigantic herds that might each include thousands of individuals. At the original Folsom site, the disposition of the bones shows that a group of 23 animals had been trapped and killed in a blind gully. Here, and at some other Folsom kills, the hunters' main object seems to have been hides rather than meat; the remains are not scattered about as they would have been if the bison had been butchered, and the tail bones, which would have come away with the hide, are nearly all missing. No doubt the hides were used for warm robes or other clothing to protect their wearers from the cold.

By Plano times the "surround" technique of the Folsom hunters had been augmented by the "jump" method—the stampeding of bison to their death over a cliff or the lip of a gully. It made game-killing possible on a truly grand scale. This method, along with the surround, was to persist among the Plains Indians well into historic times; Lewis and Clark witnessed it in 1805. That it had remained essentially unchanged over many thousands of years is indicated by a Plano kill site discovered near Kit Carson, Colorado. Here, some 10,000 years ago, a group of hunters had driven a herd of bison into a 12-foot-wide arroyo, or gully, a natural pitfall that had begun long before as a bison trail to water and had since eroded in places to a depth of seven or eight feet. So

The kill over, five of the hunters team up to pull a bison from the ravine—each bull weighed over a ton, and many animals wedged in the ravine had to be left where they died. As soon as a bison is pulled out, one man tilts the head up as another cuts open the throat (right) and severs the tender tongue—the most savoury part, which the hunters devoured raw on the spot. The carcass was then rolled over onto its belly to slit the hide down the back and get at the fatty hump.

rich in evidence was the site that the hunt itself could be reconstructed for this book in a series of precisely detailed drawings (*pages 44-53*). The dig revealed, among other things, that the hunt had taken place in late May or early June, since the skeletons unearthed include those of very young calves, usually born at that time of year. The remains even told the direction the wind was blowing that day: many animals, piled up at the bottom of the arroyo and too difficult for the Indians to remove for butchering, lay just as they had fallen, facing southwards—indicating the southerly direction of the breeze that had allowed the hunters who had stampeded them to slip in undetected. Moreover, stone points found among skeletons at the easternmost part of the death trap revealed that spearmen stationed to the north and west had kept the bison from wheeling and escaping.

Piles of bones at this site show that the Plano people butchered as efficiently as they hunted. They had systematically cut up several bison at a time, beginning with the forequarters; after stripping the meat from the bones, they had discarded them in the same order in which they had removed them from the carcasses. The bottom layer of the piles consisted of forelegs; above these lay pelvic girdles and hind legs. Next came spinal columns from most of which the meaty chest ribs had been cut away, and on top of the piles were the skulls. Scattered throughout the piles were the bison's tongue bones, indicating that the butchers—following a practice common among later Plains Indians—had cut out the tongues and eaten these delicacies raw while working.

The development of special techniques for large-scale hunting implies an important social advance among the hunters: the coalescence—at least during

With the butchering process in full swing, hunters swarm over the bloody carcasses. The six men in the centre, having slashed the skin along the backbone with their flint blades, tug at it to expose the hump and rib cage. Behind them others pile cut-up meat on a skin, while one man, arms held high, acts as garbage man and hurls a leg bone into the ravine.

the hunting season—of sizable social groupings. A mammoth or a single bison could have been killed by a dozen or so hunters, perhaps members of a single related group, but mass buffalo drives suggest the co-operation of at least several score of individuals. The archaeologists who worked on the Kit Carson site estimate that something like 60,000 pounds of meat must have been butchered there; they believe that no fewer than 150 people would have been required to carry away even a third of it.

While the Plano people continued to be dependent upon game, they also seem to have turned more and more to plants for food. The unearthing of grinding stones and slabs at Plano sites in the West and Midwest, all the way from New Mexico to Missouri, suggests that by Plano times wild plant foods had become an increasingly important part of the community's subsistence base.

Why such a shift in eating habits? The answer is tied up with one of the most hotly debated puzzles in American prehistory—the disappearance of the mammoth and many other North American big-game animals. Between about 6,000 and 12,000 years ago —a time that saw the rise of the Clovis, Folsom and Plano hunters—more than a hundred species of mammals mysteriously became extinct in North America, among them the mammoth, the mastodon, the horse and the camel, the great ground sloths and all but a modern variety of bison. (For the horse it was the second extinction in the Americas: the original American types had died out at about the time more modern types—themselves descended from American emigrants—came over the land bridge from Asia, and these modern immigrants then disappeared in Plano times, leaving the New World devoid of horses until they were reintroduced by Hernán Cortés in

*To celebrate the kill, hunters and their
families gather at a campsite where
crude shelters of hides draped over
sticks are set up. While men, women
and children feast on spitted bison
in the foreground, other Indians behind
them scrape a stretched hide and hang
strips of meat on racks to dry. The sun-
dried meat will serve as a lightweight
ration until the next successful hunt.*

*Getting ready to move on, a hunter and
his wife wrap up dried meat and their
gear in hides, and attach the bundles to
a travois, a carrying device pulled
by dogs. Poles used for shelters and
drying racks provide shafts for the
travois. In the background, a woman
carries a bundle on her back, using a
band over her head to support the load.*

the year 1518.) This same time span also saw major climate changes. With the final retreat of the ice sheets, the generally cool and moist weather that had prevailed in late glacial times gave way in many areas to warmer, drier conditions approaching those of the present.

Were the animals wiped out by man, by climate or by both? Those who hold man guilty of destroying the game by prehistoric overkill do not think that climatic changes alone can satisfactorily account for the extinctions. In the words of Professor Frank C. Hibben of the Department of Anthropology at the University of New Mexico, nothing would have prevented the beasts "from simply following the retreating ice to find just the type of vegetation and just the climate they desired. If Newport is cold in winter, go to Florida. If Washington becomes too hot in the summer, go to Maine."

More significant than climate, say the proponents of the overkill theory, is the fact that many of the extinct animals were not only large but gregarious—just those species that would have attracted hunters and been most vulnerable to their increasingly sophisticated and effective hunting techniques. The experts argue that the development of such mass slaughter methods as the jump hunt, which destroyed many more animals than could be used, may well have reduced to zero the chances of a species coming back from the brink of extinction.

Those who would exonerate the ancient big-game hunters, on the other hand, point out that similar, if less spectacular, extinctions had occurred among North American mammals long before the arrival of man. In a few cases, such as the mammoth, the hunters may have given the *coup de grâce* to a species that, for reasons still obscure, was already on na-

ture's endangered list. But while the mammoth, the long-horned bison and other large and gregarious game animals vanished, still others almost equally large and no less gregarious survived, including the modern bison, which was hunted by the jump method in Plano times and was still being hunted by the same method in the 19th Century. In fact, the bison survived in the millions even after its Indian hunters acquired firearms. The animals became virtually extinct only in the last century when bands of white hunters deliberately set out to destroy them as a means of exterminating the Indians by reducing their food supply and starving them to death.

However the great extinctions came about—at the hands of man alone or with the assistance of nature —they foreshadowed important changes in the prehistoric American way of life. One reason often proposed for the increasing reliance on plant foods is a shortage of game following the wave of extinctions. Another relates the rise of foraging to population pressure. The expansion of people during Clovis times seems to have continued during the Folsom and Plano periods. The result would have been to place narrower bounds on the wanderings of the hunting bands. No longer could they simply follow the game wherever it led, as the big-game hunters had done; now, they would eventually reach the hunting grounds of another band—which would have resented, and resisted, the intruders. Of necessity, each group would have had to make do with whatever resources its own territory offered, compensating for the narrowing of its boundaries by more intensive exploitation of the plants as well as the animals within the region. When hunters cannot hunt freely, they have no choice but to become foragers.

Chapter Three: Foragers in a Land of Plenty

Although the earliest Americans to leave definite traces were basically hunters of such big game as mammoths and long-horned bison, the continent over which they and their descendants spread was incredibly rich in other food resources, both animal and vegetable. Even after the extinction of some of the largest beasts, the plains of North America still supported an enormous population of antelope as well as bison of respectable size, and the mountains and forests abounded with deer, bear, beaver, fox, turkey and hundreds of other smaller game species. Rivers and lakes teemed with fish and, in season, attracted waterfowl in flocks that darkened the sky over the flyways. The sea coasts offered an inexhaustible supply of fish and shellfish, augmented in some places by sea otters, seals, porpoises and huge whales. And in all parts of the land, even in desert regions where game was not especially plentiful, there were at least some plant foods available for the taking—wild fruits and berries, nuts, edible roots and seeds of many kinds. Thus, without agriculture, the ancient Indians could live well even after the huge mammoth, mastodon, giant bison, dire wolf and ground sloth had finally disappeared.

That the killers of big game often settled for less spectacular foodstuffs is certain. The proof appears among the bones of mammoths and bison that were the earliest Americans' staples: at Clovis sites there are also horse and camel remains, and Folsom en-

Discovered in a cave in western Utah, this fragment of a 6,000-year-old net pouch testifies to the ingenuity of prehistoric man in America as he turned from big-game hunting to foraging for plants and small animals. Desert dwellers wove the pouch from fibres of milkweed stems and probably used it like a shopping bag to carry the foods they gathered.

campments have yielded bones of foxes and deer. In the camps of the later Plano bison hunters there are stones unmistakably shaped for grinding, evidence that Plano men varied their meat diet with some sort of processed plant product. It may be that all these hunting peoples depended more on vegetable foods than is indicated by the remains of their meals. Animal bones tossed aside after a hunt feast can survive for thousands of years, but vegetable debris usually decomposes in a few weeks.

The shift from a life style focused on big game to a broader economy based on the exploitation of a variety of plant and animal foods—foraging as opposed to hunting—becomes clearer in the stage of North American prehistory called the Archaic, which reached its height some 7,000 years ago.

That it was a change in degree more than in kind is apparent in the tool kits left by the peoples of Archaic times. In nearly all of them the hunter's stone spear point is still a prominent item, but now there is a variety of tools. Technical sophistication is apparent in special tools for spearing, hooking, netting and trapping fish. Stone itself comes into broad use in a new form—tools that are ground rather than chipped. This change in manufacturing process was much more than a refinement, for it enormously expanded the supplies of raw materials available for toolmaking. Almost any tough stone, such as basalt, could now be formed into a serviceable axe while an easily split material like slate, which cannot readily be chipped like flint, could be ground into a very creditable spearhead, and chunks of soft stone could be hollowed out to make vessels. And from this period comes the first evidence of widespread use of a number of significant inventions: boats, woven baskets as well as cloth, and even some objects of metal.

Many of these great leaps in technology seem to have taken place some 9,000 years ago. From Danger Cave, on the western edge of Great Salt Desert in Utah, come a surprising variety of ancient artifacts. There are darts, awls, millstones and mica discs. Most significant to a foraging people, who need strong but lightweight containers for collecting seeds and nuts, are remnants of twined and coiled cords—almost a certain indication that the inhabitants of Danger Cave knew how to weave baskets. Since basketry ordinarily decays fairly rapidly, the Indians may well have learned the art of weaving even earlier —in the opinion of some experts, they were the first people in the entire world to master this priceless skill. And with the use of a wholly new material, copper, the ancient Indians took the first tentative steps towards the age of metal.

The size and complexity of the tool kit and the changes such gear produced in its owners' way of life varied according to where they lived. Environment was everywhere the controlling factor. In the western deserts, resources were sparser. Men were compelled to maintain a nomadic existence to find enough food for survival, and their possessions were largely limited to what they could carry on their backs. In richer areas, such as some of the eastern woodlands, more plentiful resources ready at hand made possible the appearance of little settlements, more or less permanent base camps for extended foraging expeditions, and also led to the accumulation of greater numbers of tools. And in one region, the Northwest Coast, a combination of magnificent natural resources and a highly efficient technology for harvesting them eventually produced truly permanent villages, complete with planked houses, paddle-propelled war canoes more than 50 feet long, decorative paintings and carvings, and a strikingly elaborate ceremonial life. Here, in what is now Oregon, Washington, southeast Alaska, British Columbia and northern California, prospered one of the most luxuriant preagricultural societies the world has ever known.

The first evidence of the transition from big-game hunting to a foraging life comes from the desert country lying between the Rockies and the Sierra Nevada and Cascade ranges. This huge area, where large game animals probably were never numerous, is mostly plateau and includes all of Nevada, Utah and Arizona and arid or semiarid parts of Oregon, Idaho, California, western New Mexico and much of northern Mexico. It is one of the most rigorous habitats in North America, imposing severe limitations on human existence. The great mountain ranges to west and east, their peaks topping 14,000 feet, trap most of the moisture moving in from the Pacific and up from the Gulf of Mexico. On the plateau between, precipitation averages around 10 inches a year and not much more than that on top of the mountains that seam the plateau with north-to-south ridges.

Though the region contains a few large rivers—the Snake to the north, the Green-Colorado-Gila system to the south—these watercourses flow through precipitous canyons (the Colorado's mile-deep Grand Canyon being the champion), and their isolation from the surrounding countryside minimizes their overall influence on the vegetation as well as their accessibility to man. Elsewhere, the streams descend from the mountains only to lose themselves in desert sand or stagnant "sinks"; often they vanish altogether in the hot season. There are only a few lakes, and most of these are brackish or, like Great Salt Lake, even saltier than the oceans; some disappear temporarily after a run of dry years.

Vegetation varies somewhat from north to south, but much more with altitude and proximity to water: reeds, rushes, grass, herbs, scrubby willows and an occasional cottonwood along the banks of lake or stream; sagebrush, greasewood and scattered tufts of hardy grasses on the drier flats. In the southern deserts are cacti ranging from pincushion size to the majestic saguaro, towering 30 feet or more in the air. On the mountains are open stands of piñon and juniper, giving way, on the very highest peaks, to groves of lodgepole pine, alpine meadows and finally permanent snow fields.

According to geologists, this rugged region was once somewhat moister, supporting more vegetation and wildlife than it does today. The animal life was then diversified: some bison and elk in the most favoured sections north and east, but elsewhere nothing larger than deer and bighorn sheep on the high mountain slopes; lower down the biggest game was pronghorn antelope; but the commonest animals were such unobtrusive species as rabbit, marmot, prairie dog and wood rat. Only seldom and under exceptional conditions were these animals ever plentiful enough to supply more than a small part of prehistoric man's rations; for the most part, the desert dweller had to eat anything he could find.

The oldest evidence of the beginning of this eclectic diet was found in Ventana Cave, south of Phoenix in the sagebrush, yucca and cactus desert of southern Arizona. The people who lived in this cave were relatives of the Clovis hunters—in the deepest layers of the cave floor, dating back some 10,000 or 11,000 years, a small Clovis point was found. Yet unlike their mammoth-hunting neighbours, Ventana men were not hunters of big game; many of the bones associated with their weapons are of small animals such as deer, coyotes, peccaries and badgers.

These people had already learned to make good use of the most common of desert vegetation—the seeds of grasses and shrubs. In one of the cave's lower levels was a relatively flat stone with a slightly concave surface. It looks like a grinding stone and is probably the oldest example of the tool that is a hallmark of most North American foragers. With such a stone, the seeds of grasses, indigestible in their raw state, can be ground up and then cooked to make the gruel and unleavened bread that even today sustains many people of the southwestern deserts.

From other digs have come not only grinding stones nearly as old as Ventana Cave's, but also traces of baskets—the implement that fills the seed-eaters' need for cooking utensils and for easily portable containers to permit efficient harvesting of the wild crops. With stone grinding tools and lightweight woven baskets, the desert food-gatherers were now equipped with the basic kit for exploiting their environment's most reliable food supply.

Among people who are essentially hunters, seeds constitute a fallback resource when game is scarce. And in the North American desert, game was frequently scarce and generally small, so that the economy of its inhabitants came to centre largely around seeds. Seeds collected in baskets included those of such plants as pickleweed, sunflower and yucca, and ranged in size from acorns found in a few relatively moist places to tiny Indian millet seeds found in the desert. Placed on the surface of a grinding stone and ground with a small, bun-shaped stone held in the hand, the seeds were reduced to coarse meal; the meal was then formed into cakes to be baked in ashes or boiled up into a mush in watertight baskets into which hot stones were dropped. It was this primitive milling equipment developed by the Archaic desert people that provided the prototypes of the metate and mano still widely used in rural households of Mexico to grind cultivated corn.

People living on seeds and small game rapidly came to occupy nearly all the arid and semiarid region west of the Rockies from Oregon into Mexico. Subsequently, simple agriculture developed in the southern part of this region, but north of the river Colorado, where harsh geography combined with harsh climate to limit progress and foster conservatism, the foraging way of life persisted without radical change from at least 7500 B.C. until historic times. The Shoshoni, Ute and Paiute tribes, confined by their stronger neighbours to the Great Basin—a rugged area that includes Utah's Great Salt Lake, the wastelands of Nevada and Death Valley in California—were still hard-pressed desert foragers when first encountered by white explorers. Eyewitness accounts of the habits of these tribes, supplemented by the evidence of materials discovered by archaeologists, permit reconstruction of the lives of the desert tribes' prehistoric predecessors —or perhaps ancestors.

The scene is the northwest corner of what is now Utah, where flat desert country merges with steep, bare mountains. The time is early spring, around 4,000 years ago. A band of desert people is moving down from a mountain valley where it has passed the winter in the company of a few other bands—all related by blood or marriage and making up a very loosely structured tribe. During winter the oily, aromatic nuts provided by groves of piñon pine had been the tribe's principal food. But now the store of piñon nuts has been exhausted, and each band must search elsewhere for food. Like the other groups, this one descending the mountain slopes is small, including no more than 20 or 30 people of a single large family and of all ages—wrinkled grandparents, sturdy adults and tiny toddlers strapped to their mothers' backs. Trotting along beside them are their dogs, animals that by now have been domesticated in America for at least 6,000 years and serve as valuable aids in hunting, as scavengers about the camp, as an early warning system against the approach of animal or human predators—and as a source of food.

The sun is brilliant as the band nears the desert floor, but this early in the year a wintry chill still hangs in the air for much of the day, so that both men and women wear fur blankets or robes clutched or belted about them; for protection against the rocky desert soil they wear rush-woven sandals, since tough hides for moccasins are hard to come by.

Arriving at the bank of a small, shallow river—the only one within their territory—they set up a temporary camp. The men haul lines and bone hooks from their packs, bait them with scraps of meat and cast them into the deeper pools in search of trout, suckers or bullheads. Meanwhile, the women cut young shoots of thistle, watercress, squaw cabbage and clover for a meal of the greens that the band has missed all winter; others get out their pointed hardwood digging sticks to unearth the still-tender rootstocks of bulrushes, which line the swampier portions of the stream bank. On the flats away from the river, some teenage boys encourage the dogs to scare up a jack rabbit or two that they can use as practice targets for their throwing sticks and for darts hurled by an atlatl, or spear thrower. They do not yet have bows and arrows, which will not appear in America for another 10 centuries.

In a few weeks, the men know, ducks will pass through on their way to northern nesting grounds, and it is time for the men to make an expedition to the small, landlocked lake, some 12 miles downstream, where their river comes to an end. The lake is brackish, but not lifeless, and the migrating birds stop by for worms and insect larvae.

In a sandstone ledge above the lake is a small cave that has long served the Indians as a cache for equipment too heavy or bulky to be carried during their nomadic wanderings each year. The men haul out a set of realistic decoys, made of reeds sewn together with fibre thread and covered with duck feathers. For several days the hunters wait each morning and evening, hidden in the patches of reeds that grow along the lakeside, until finally a flight of ducks spies the decoys and lands on the lake to feed. As the birds swim closer to the lifelike decoys, the men suddenly leap up and fling their darts; most of the birds take off in fright but half a dozen are down, to be brought ashore by the dogs, which can expect the guts as a reward. Meanwhile, a few boys who had begged to come along on the hunt search the reedy shallows for eggs of grebes or mud hens, or set fibre-cord snares for wood rats and rabbits.

When the last skein of ducks has passed through, the hunters return their decoys to the cache and after resting a day, pull out a fishing net, also of fibre cord and weighted along the bottom edge with stones. Six or seven of them wade out waist deep, then bring the net around in a loop with its harvest of fish.

By late spring the fierce sun pushes afternoon temperatures well above the 38°C. mark, and the river beside the band's base camp has shrunk to a string of pools joined by trickles of water or stretches of damp sand. The men are now stripped down to antelope-skin breechcloths; the women wear no more than short aprons of hide, one in front, the other in back. To provide shade during the midday heat, the people build shelters of brush. These huts afford little protection against the pelting drops of a thunderstorm, but rain is very rare and so brief that within minutes the hot sun dries up the puddles.

It is now the time for the women to scour the desert for roots and tubers, their tall, conical collecting baskets of willow splints, reeds or grass (some hold more than a bushel) set on their backs and braced by a strap that passes around the forehead. Among the roots and tubers they dig are bitter-root, camas, sago and yampa, many of which will be stored. Now, as the season advances, it is time to begin collecting the seeds of ripening rice grass, pickleweed and other plants. They are carefully tapped into a small basket held in one hand and the small basket is periodically emptied into a larger one. Back at camp, the seeds are roasted by being shaken with live coals in wickerwork trays; the heat splits the inedible husks and frees the seeds inside. When the roasting is completed, the women, with a dexterous twirl of the tray, separate coals from seeds. Part of the crop is then ground up for immediate use in cakes or as mush, the women rubbing away at their grinding stones, chattering

Versatile Basketry: Containers for Foragers

Once the ancient Indians began to switch from meat to plants for their staple food, they needed a new kind of implement: baskets to hold nuts, seeds and berries. The techniques of basketry soon made possible other useful things, such as hats, sandals and fish traps and even objects of ceremonial and aesthetic value.

Only fragments of the earliest baskets survive, but these later examples, assembled from the collections of The Museum of the American Indian in New York and the Smithsonian Institution, are believed to follow ancient designs. Work baskets include (*left to right*): a Cape Cod Mashpee carrying basket with a strap; a California grinding basket of fibres coiled on top of a mortar stone; an Apache storage basket; a southwestern water bottle, waterproofed with pine gum; and a "wallet" basket, used by northwestern Wasco Indians for carrying personal possessions.

CARRYING BASKET

GRINDING BASKET

WALLET BASKET

WATER BOTTLE

STORAGE BASKET

Basketry: Hats, Trays, Decoys

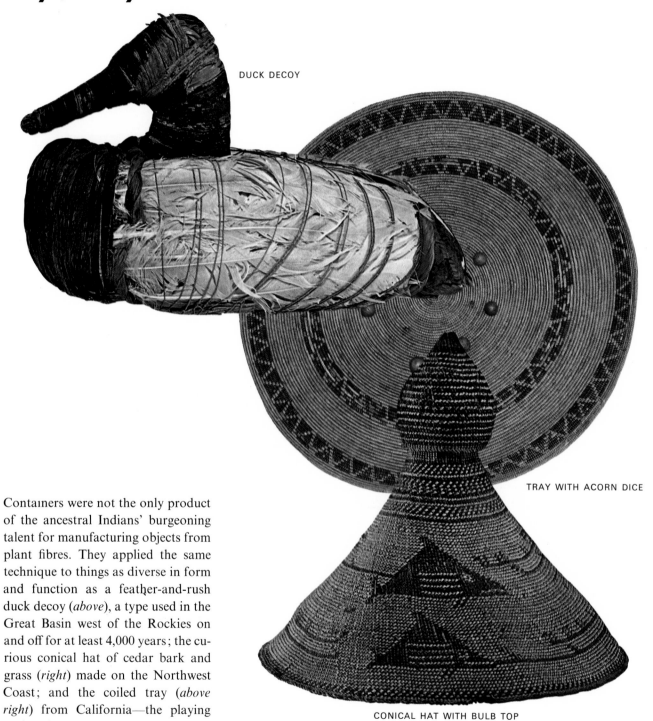

DUCK DECOY

TRAY WITH ACORN DICE

CONICAL HAT WITH BULB TOP

Containers were not the only product of the ancestral Indians' burgeoning talent for manufacturing objects from plant fibres. They applied the same technique to things as diverse in form and function as a feather-and-rush duck decoy (*above*), a type used in the Great Basin west of the Rockies on and off for at least 4,000 years; the curious conical hat of cedar bark and grass (*right*) made on the Northwest Coast; and the coiled tray (*above right*) from California—the playing surface for an ancient gambling game employing dice made of pitch-stuffed acorns marked with abalone shell.

with one another or keeping time to a chant that one of them sings out. The remaining seeds are kept for future use in deep, jug-shaped baskets.

Meanwhile, the band's hunters have not been idle with their snares, traps and spear throwers. Antelopes, in particular, are unusually abundant this year, so some of the meat can be cut into strips and preserved by drying in the sun instead of being roasted and eaten immediately.

Early autumn brings berry season, with elderberry, chokecherry, buffalo berry, wild currant and serviceberry beginning to ripen along the banks of the shrunken river. With these crops gathered, it is time for the band to move back towards the mountains, for in late autumn the piñon nuts—the principal winter food resource of these people—are ready to be harvested. The band cannot, however, return to its last winter's quarters, for the piñon groves there are exhausted and will not yield another abundant crop for three or four years. But during the previous winter, hunting parties had noted a ridge where the cones were growing well enough to promise a rich harvest this autumn. It is to this previously selected winter campground that the band now travels.

As the band approaches the piñon ridge, smoke rising in the autumn air announces that another group is there before it, attracted not only by nourishing piñon nuts but by anticipation of an important co-operative activity—a rabbit hunt. Soon the ridge is occupied by half a dozen bands, and the outlook is encouraging; the spokesman for one of the groups reports that the rabbit population of a near-by valley shows a marked increase this season. The carrier of this news is the boss of the rabbit drive, a position he holds mainly through his family's possession of

an unusually long rabbit net. This remarkable object, woven of milkweed-fibre cordage, resembles a coarse-meshed fish net, but is less than two feet wide. It is more than 200 feet long, however, having been added to bit by bit over half a dozen generations. When a dozen similar nets owned by other families and nearly as long are attached to it, the resulting mesh will stretch over a half mile.

The rabbit hunt involves the combined forces of all the assembled bands—only the aged and mothers with babies are left behind. An advance party quietly makes its way to the mouth of the rabbit valley to tie together the sections of net and set it up, while the rest prepare to serve as beaters. They distribute themselves along the tops of the steep ridges that wall the valley on either side, and at a smoke signal from the leader begin to move downhill. As the shouting men thrash the underbrush with sticks, their deep voices are echoed by the shriller tones of the boys and yelps of the dogs.

A jack rabbit takes off down the valley in four-foot leaps—then three more rabbits break cover, then a dozen. In 20 minutes the upper valley is alive with bounding animals. Meanwhile, the advance party has lined up in front of the net, ready with their clubs and throwing sticks. As the first stampeding rabbits approach, the hunters try to kill as many as possible short of the net, since too many rabbits striking the light fibre cords at once could tear them. A second line of hunters disposes of animals entangled in the meshes, and catches many of those that manage to get through or over it.

By the time the last of the beaters reaches the net, the ground around it is heaped with the furry prey. After a pause for breath, the hunters begin skinning and cleaning the animals with flint blades. With the meat they go back to camp where, after a rabbit feast, the women take up the job of dressing the skins. Beginning at the outer edge of a spread-out pelt and cutting around and around in spiral fashion towards the centre; the women convert the skins into long strips; a skilful cutter can make one up to 20 feet long. The strips are then stretched between trees until they are dry and the edges curl inwards, the result being a furry rope up to an inch thick. Thirty or so six-foot lengths of rope, stretched closely side by side and tied together at about a dozen places with bits of skin, make a thick rabbitskin blanket.

It is none too soon, for the days are rapidly growing shorter and colder. Already the more provident families have dug circular pits in the ground and roofed them over with saplings, boughs and hides or bark. In these pit huts they will spend the long winter months, sustained largely by air-dried meat and their stores of roots, seeds and piñon nuts. Soon the mountains are blanketed in snow for weeks on end —a time for mending nets and other hunting gear, for making new equipment, for furthering social ties and for storytelling around the smoky fires. But all too soon the precious supply of food dwindles, and an occasional beaver, deer or wildcat brought in by the hunters is not sufficient to quiet a growing hunger. When at last lengthening days signal the approach of spring, the assembled groups waste no time before splitting up into bands and beginning the seasonal round of foraging once more.

Outside the western desert regions, most Archaic foragers had an easier life. In central California, where oak groves were large and plentiful, the main crop

FEATHER-TRIMMED STORAGE BASKET

Basketry: Works of Art and Ritual

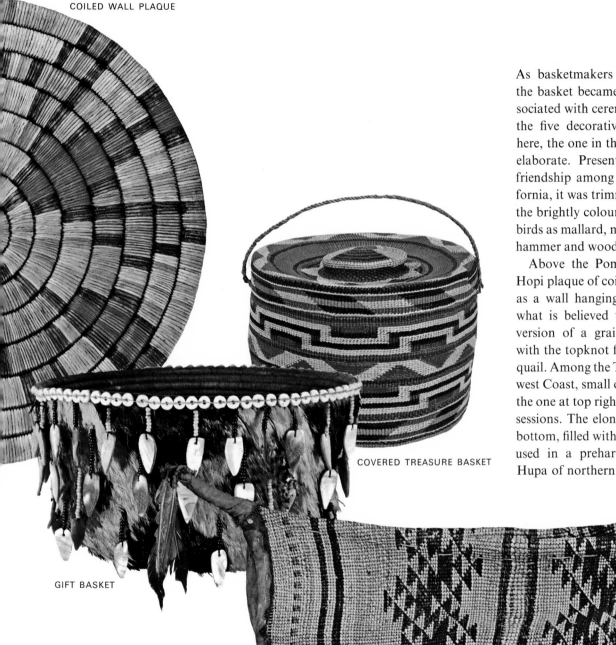

COILED WALL PLAQUE

COVERED TREASURE BASKET

GIFT BASKET

JUMP DANCE BASKET

As basketmakers grew more skilful the basket became a work of art, associated with ceremony and ritual. Of the five decorative examples shown here, the one in the centre is the most elaborate. Presented as a token of friendship among the Pomo of California, it was trimmed with shells and the brightly coloured feathers of such birds as mallard, meadow lark, yellow hammer and woodpecker.

Above the Pomo gift basket is a Hopi plaque of coiled yucca, designed as a wall hanging, and to its left is what is believed to be a dressed-up version of a grain basket, trimmed with the topknot feathers of the male quail. Among the Tlingit of the Northwest Coast, small covered baskets like the one at top right held precious possessions. The elongated basket at the bottom, filled with sacred objects, was used in a preharvest dance by the Hupa of northern California.

was acorns, which the women gathered by the bushel, shelled, ground, then soaked in pools in shallow sand pits to remove the tannic acid that gives a strong bitter taste to gruel or bread made from untreated acorn flour. A little farther westward were the rich food resources of the California sea coast—abalones, clams, mussels, many kinds of fish and such marine mammals as seals and sea otters. In both of these well-provisioned areas, the foraging groups were larger than in the desert, and life tended to centre around more or less permanent base camps.

On the Great Plains east of the Rockies, there were so many buffalo that hunting continued as a principal source of food, and the people remained largely nomadic, tracking the great herds much as they had done in Folsom and Plano times. Beyond the plains, the forest country stretching to the Atlantic was unsuited to such easily caught large herd animals; the chief game was deer, but those who hunted it did not scorn wildcat, turkey, squirrel, opossum, terrapin and a variety of fresh-water fish and mussels, as well as acorns, hickory nuts and walnuts. Postholes found at a few of their sites indicate that some of the woodland residents were constructing fairly elaborate dwellings and so must have been considerably more settled than the desert or plains people. Moreover, enormous heaps of fresh-water shells in Kentucky and Tennessee point to a population that was not only more settled but more numerous.

As the foragers multiplied and settled down, they developed increasingly specialized tools and techniques. Most forest dwellers had extensive kits of specialized gear: axes, drills, gouges and other woodworking tools of ground or chipped stone, fishhooks, harpoons, nets (for game and fowl as well as fish),

plus mortars and pestles for crushing plant foods. But some foragers were even more ingenious, inventing wholly new equipment and processes that were to play key rôles in later Indian life.

In one small area, just west of the Great Lakes, metal came into use. Tools as well as ornaments were hammered out of naturally pure copper nuggets found near by. This metalwork, begun some 5,000 years ago, seems to have been the first in the New World—preceding even the gold and silver smelting of South America—but though the products were ingeniously designed and eventually became important goods in the Indians' wide-ranging commerce, the methods of the Great Lakes smiths remained rudimentary. The copper workers never learned to cast metal, as the peoples of Mexico and other centres of Indian civilization later did; nor did they learn to smelt copper, chemically treating the compounds of ores so that they released their copper components in metallic form. The pioneer craft was restricted to the small area where pieces of pure metal could be found ready to use.

The general area west of the Great Lakes—the densely forested North Woods that stretch from Wisconsin and Minnesota into Canada—also could have been the birthplace of one of the most important of Indian inventions, the birchbark canoe. It is certain that such a craft must have been particularly useful in this area, where thousands of big and little lakes are interconnected by a network of streams and rivers, but there are gaps in the interconnections. Only a lightweight craft can navigate the often shallow streams and be easily carried across portages between waterways. Once available, the bark canoe opened up the otherwise impenetrable North Woods;

it converted the region's web of lakes and streams into routes of commerce.

Along the Atlantic sea coast, another food resource —fish—stimulated Indian ingenuity. Here the fish were not merely hooked and netted; they were also trapped, and sometimes apparently in immense quantities. One huge fish trap, or weir, discovered 60 years ago during excavations in Boston, was built about 2000 B.C. The enclosure extended over two acres of what was then a shallow lagoon. Its building required an estimated 65,000 stakes, sharpened with stone axes and set in double rows and interlaced with brush. The labour involved in such a construction shows that it was not intended for sporadic or even brief, seasonal use. Rather, it implies a fairly large, settled population—and one sufficiently well organized to permit the building and use of such an extensive installation.

The richest and most highly developed of the foraging Indians, however, were not to be found on the Atlantic seaboard, in the eastern woodlands or in bountiful central California, but along the Northwest Coast. Here, on a 2,000-mile strip of shore—including part of Alaska and stretching southwards through British Columbia, Washington, Oregon and into the northern tip of California—arose a rare kind of culture, one that was very advanced despite the absence of farming. The food resources—especially those of river and sea—were so abundant that the people could provide for their needs by foraging no farther afield than their doorsteps.

The extravagance of the natural bounty not only raised the possibility of life in permanent villages, it created a positive necessity for it; as one anthropol-ogist has dryly observed, "even a large family group is unlikely to favour a nomadic way of life if they have half a ton of dried salmon to lug around with them". The fact that the half ton of salmon—food for several months—could be caught and processed in a couple of weeks' intensive work and used to feed a large population over several months also meant freedom to develop nonsubsistence activities. The result was a proliferation of arts, crafts, ceremonies and rituals of a vigour and elaborateness unsurpassed in ancient North America.

The remarkable foraging culture of the Northwest Coast prospered so because of an unusual natural setting. From east to west, hemmed between the Pacific Ocean on one side and the Coast Mountains of British Columbia and the Cascades of Washington and Oregon on the other, the region is seldom as much as a hundred miles wide. The ocean, warmed by the Japan Current, moistens and tempers the prevailing westerly winds, while even in winter the mountains block off most cold air from the interior, at the same time intensifying precipitation: as the moist oceanic winds rise, approaching the mountains, they are chilled so that their moisture condenses and falls. Thus, lush green covers the strip west of the mountains; to the east is desert.

In prehistoric times the entire region was densely forested—parts of the Puget Sound country, in fact, still support one of the world's few temperate-zone rain forests, a wet expanse lushly overgrown with spruce, pine and cedar shooting up 150 to 200 feet, topped by the majestic, 250-foot Douglas fir. Around the fringes of this dense, almost impenetrable evergreen forest, large game such as deer and moose and several varieties of bear was reasonably abundant, and in the mountains lived mountain goat and sheep.

But the sea was, by far, a richer resource, providing whale, porpoise, seal, sea lion, sea otter, halibut up to a quarter-ton each and sturgeon twice as large, shoals of herring and smelt, and the extraordinary eulachon, or candlefish, so oily when dried that a string threaded through it burns like a wick. The tidal flats yielded such fare as the enormous geoduck clam, half a dozen of which would make a meal for a large family, while in spring and autumn clouds of migrating waterfowl challenged the hunter's guile.

But richest of all resources were the rivers. As often as seven times a year, spawning salmon filled the waters with leaping, silvery fish that could be speared, netted or trapped by the ton, and then dried or smoked for future use. No people who had learned to exploit these resources need often have gone hungry, even in the depth of winter.

The nature of the region's resources ensured that its inhabitants would be largely based on the coast and their life orientated towards the sea—an orientation that in most places was strengthened by the topography of the land itself. From Puget Sound northwards, the mountains rise steeply from the sea, and the coast is cut by deep fjords, gouged out by ice-age glaciers whose remnants flow down from the peaks even in the 20th Century, and studded with islands ranging in size from pin points of rock to the 285-mile-long Vancouver Island. In such country, land travel for more than a few miles was always difficult and in most places physically impossible; with boats, however, men could move with ease and tolerable safety among protected channels, at the same time exploiting the marine life.

The earliest inhabitants of this Eden lived 8,000 years ago on the lower river Columbia between Washington and Oregon and also near the mouth of the Fraser in British Columbia, where they hunted seals as well as land animals. But not until about 1000 B.C. was the extravagant life peculiar to the Northwest Coast established. It arose among people apparently related to the ancestral Eskimos, descendants of relatively recent arrivals from Asia, who at around the same period were developing a distinctive maritime hunting culture in the Far North.

The evidence for a family connection lies in both anatomy and customs. When the Northwest Coast Indians were first studied in the 19th Century, they turned out to have a higher incidence than other Indians of the "Mongoloid fold" that makes Oriental eyes appear slanted, arguing for a possible infusion of Mongoloid genes from early Eskimos and Aleuts. In addition, artifacts discovered along the coast and dating from around 1000 B.C. include such typically Eskimo tools as semicircular knives of ground slate and toggle harpoons, the kind that have pivoted heads to turn in a wound so they cannot slip out.

But despite links to the ancestral Eskimos, the Northwest Indians developed a life that was uniquely their own. Its great wealth was based on the wealth of the environment, which provided not only a surfeit of food but also an array of raw materials for many purposes, utilitarian and otherwise.

In such densely forested country, the main material was wood—above all that of yellow and red cedar, which while durable was soft enough to be easily worked with stone or bone adzes and chisels. As straight logs, hand-split planks, cut chunks and pounded bark fibre, it was transformed into the prized possessions of a materialistic society.

Abstract Art for a Blanket

One prized possession exchanged by Northwest Coast Indians in the gift-giving ritual known as the potlatch was the Chilkat blanket, a fringed ceremonial robe bearing the animal crest of its owner—here a bird.

Intricately woven of mountain goat wool and cedar bark fibre, the design suggests abstractions by Picasso and Braque. Like their cubist paintings it combines multiple perspectives: the animal is rendered as though split down the middle and stretched out flat to give an overall view, and some parts are repeated. The bird's eyes appear in pairs at the top near the centre; the facelike portion in the centre is its body; the double-eye symbols on either side are the wings; and the clawed feet are at the bottom.

Cedar logs, hollowed with fire and adzes, could be stretched into canoe shape by partially filling them with heated water to soften the wood. They were built in many sizes: small ones for travel on streams, larger ones for fishing—and by some tribes for whaling—and great 60-foot-long ones for trade, warfare and ceremonial visits. Cedar logs also became the medium of these Indians' famous art form, totem poles. Ornately carved with figures of men, animals and supernatural beings, the towering poles were erected to honour dead chiefs, to mark the graves of important persons or, with doorways cut into their bases, to serve as portals to houses.

Cedar built the houses as well: the logs were split into planks with hardwood or antler wedges and cleverly grooved or notched so that they could be joined without pegs. The result was a handsome rectangular dwelling 60 feet long and 50 feet wide, its gabled roof supported on enormous cedar beams held up by massive cedar posts. While most of these houses were designed to be permanent structures, others —thanks to their pegless construction—could be easily dismantled whenever their owners had reason to do so. Such take-apart dwellings were common among Northwest Coast Indians, who customarily set up housekeeping at several fishing sites in the course of a year. At each site they maintained a house frame, and when moving time came, it was a simple matter to strip the cedar siding and roof planks from one frame and apply them to another.

Cedar planks even provided the boxes that were cherished home furnishings. They were ingeniously made: a board was cut to a cross shape, then scored so that the side pieces could be folded up into place and pegged or sewn together. Fitted with covers, smoothed with sandstone or sharkskin abrasive and usually intricately painted or carved, such containers stored almost everything from whale, seal or candlefish oil to sinew cords and spare points for arrows.

Chunks of cedar were carved into ceremonial masks—conventionalized yet vivid representations of men and beasts, equipped sometimes with leather hinges and strings by which the mouths could be opened to reveal another mask inside.

Even the bark of cedar had multiple uses. Its tough fibres were woven into blankets, into mats for covering the walls and floors of houses, into openwork baskets for carrying fish, or baskets so tightly made that they held water.

Wood, while the major raw material, was only one among many others inventively used, such as strands of kelp, which were twisted into fishlines, and the horn of mountain sheep, which was carved into spoons or steamed and spread to make bowls.

Like many other affluent peoples, the Northwest Indians eventually became obsessed with their wealth. They raised ostentatious consumption to an extreme rarely seen anywhere. In a spectacular ceremony called a potlatch—a lavish revel similar to modern parties notable for their extravagance—they gave away huge supplies of valuables to cement friendships and demonstrate status.

Custodian of the community's wealth was its principal chief, who on ceremonial occasions bestowed the surplus upon a gathering of distinguished guests. The recipients were expected to share their bounty with their own following and were obligated to stage a reciprocal gift-giving ceremony at some future time. Who the recipients of these gifts might be was rigidly regulated by family relationships based on tribal groups, called moieties (*pages 72-74*), within which intermarriage was forbidden. A potlatch could be staged for an unrelated group, or for a group to which the chief's wife belonged, but not for members of the chief's own moiety.

The purpose of a potlatch was the same as that of conspicuous consumption in modern society. Partly it increased the prestige of the chief's community, and partly it proved the chief's own status. Occasions for such demonstrations of wealth came frequently. The heir of a tribe's greatest chief had to justify his right to his post by a potlatch, or a chief might celebrate the coming of age of his eldest son, commemorate the death of another chief or dedicate the new house of an important man.

In prehistoric times potlatches were generally expansive gift-giving ceremonies—a distribution of goods meant to bring status to the donor. But after contact with Europeans had disrupted traditional society, in which hierarchical standing was more or less fixed, potlatches tended to become bitterly competitive affairs as individual chiefs, or even rich commoners who aspired to chieftainship, vied for rank. The gifts became fantastically lavish. And in some cases one man strove to belittle another by destroying valuable property and thus suggesting that his own wealth was unlimited—the Indian equivalent of lighting cigars with ten-dollar bills. Nor was such destruction necessarily limited to purely material possessions. In vaunting his wealth before a rival, a potlatch-giver would sometimes sacrifice a number of slaves, ordering them bludgeoned to death with a special club called a slave-killer and using the corpses as rollers to beach his rival's canoe. Before

the potlatch became perverted so, 18th Century explorers had opportunities to witness ceremonies in which the original communal character remained. From their accounts it is possible to imagine what a potlatch was like in A.D. 1400 or 1500, at the height of the Northwest Indian power.

The moving spirit and central figure of the season's most notable potlatch is the supreme chief of a group of island villages situated south of what will one day be Juneau, Alaska. The occasion is the raising of a portal pole before the chief's new house, a pole 12 feet tall and four feet across, completely covered with carved and painted figures symbolizing the house owner's lineage, status and titles: squatting, staring-eyed human shapes, a conventionalized killer whale and above them a ferocious eagle. The bottom of the pole is pierced with a large, elliptical hole that will be the ceremonial entrance to the house when the pole is erected.

Both the portal pole and the house it will adorn are the gifts of the guests of the potlatch—the chief's in-laws, members of his wife's moiety—and the ceremony pays them back. During the months they have spent felling and splitting trees, carving and building, the chief and his own moiety have housed and fed the workers and their families. Now the chief and his followers must contribute the huge quantities of food for the feast that will precede the gift-giving. Even the lowliest commoner contributes to the utmost of his ability, knowing that he will share in the distribution of presents when his chief is on the receiving end of some later potlatch. As this wealth accumulates there is much coming and going between the chief's home village and its neighbours,

A Social Order Based on Women of the Family

Most Indian societies were organized on strict lines of kinship that grew more elaborate when the Indians turned to foraging or agriculture and began settling down, as can be seen in the tribal structure (*below*) and the marriage arrangements (*overleaf*) of the affluent Tlingit Indians of the Pacific Northwest.

The basic social unit was not the nuclear family as it is known today in modern America, but the female side of it, called the lineage, which included a mother, her children, her broth-

Lineage

Clan

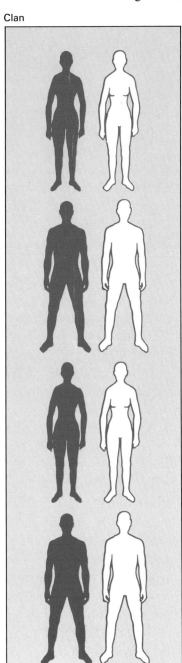

Moiety

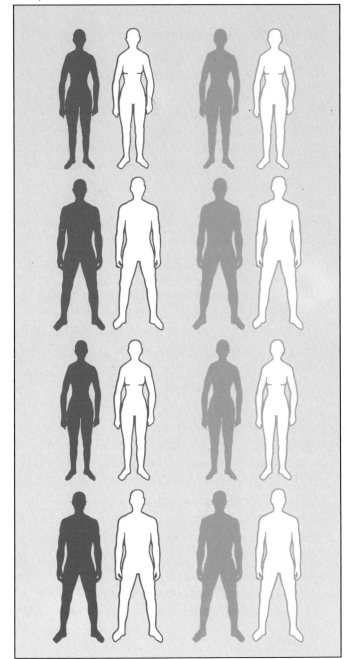

The nuclear unit of a tribe, the matrilineal kin called a lineage, is shown in the left box. The union of two lineages with a common

ers, her sisters and her sisters' offspring. The male side of the Tlingit family—the husband, his brothers, sisters and sisters' children—always belonged to another lineage.

Two or more lineages formed the clan, whose members were linked by the belief that they had a common ancestor. The clans were identified by a "totem" symbol, often an animal. A group of clans made up a "moiety"; two moieties—called the Raven and the Wolf, possibly after clan names —constituted the Tlingit tribe itself.

Lineage derived from the mother automatically bestowed rights and privileges upon members: it told each Tlingit who he was, where he could fish, what his totemic symbols were, where he could live and, most important, whom he could marry.

Tribe

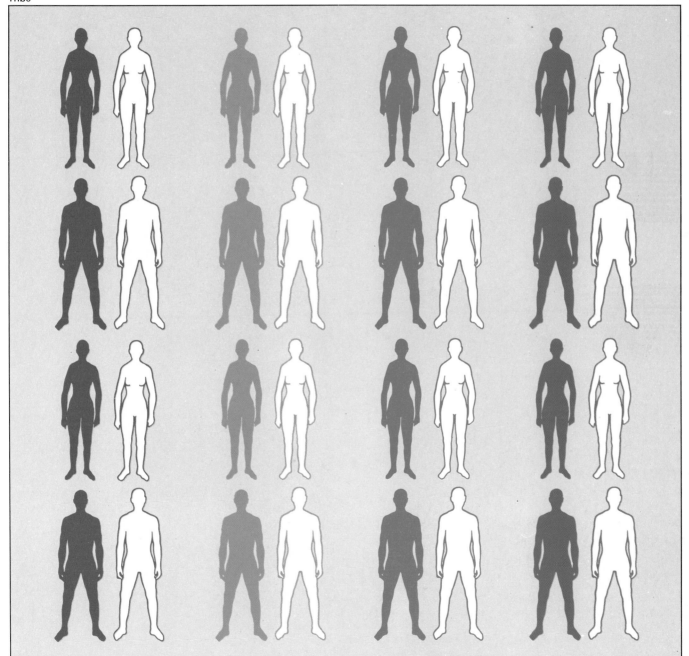

background becomes a clan (second box). Two or more clans constitute a moiety (third box); two moieties make up a tribe (above).

Matchmaking by the Rules of Kinship

In the complex society of the Tlingit Indians, who married whom was predetermined by their moiety, a tie that depended on the lineage and clan of the mother (*preceding pages*). Marriage within a moiety—a Raven to a Raven or a Wolf to a Wolf—was prohibited, and to prevent romantic slip-ups, a boy and girl in the same moiety were forbidden to speak to each other, even if they were cousins.

But the Tlingit marriages that were permitted—inter-moiety Raven-Wolf matches—also mated couples who were related by blood. They are called "cross cousins"—the father of one related to the mother of the other, as shown in the diagram below.

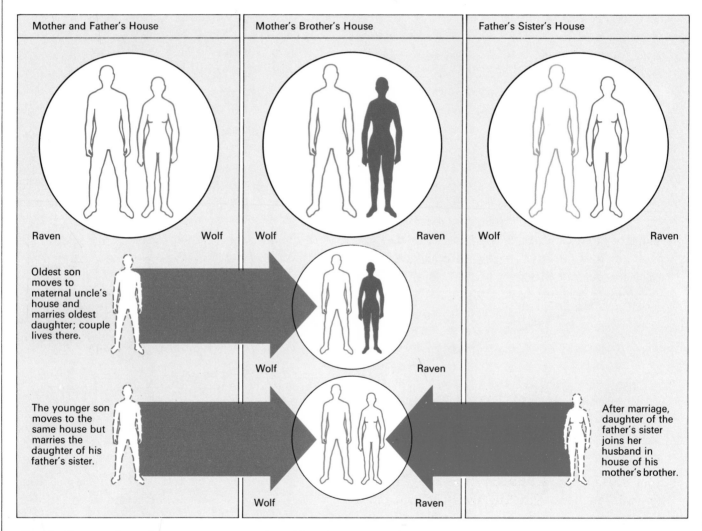

Mother and Father's House | Mother's Brother's House | Father's Sister's House

Raven — Wolf

Wolf — Raven

Wolf — Raven

Oldest son moves to maternal uncle's house and marries oldest daughter; couple lives there.

Wolf — Raven

The younger son moves to the same house but marries the daughter of his father's sister.

Wolf — Raven

After marriage, daughter of the father's sister joins her husband in house of his mother's brother.

How the Tlingit made matches among children of three couples (large circles) without marriage within a moiety is shown here. Each person is labelled with his moiety—Raven or Wolf. At age 10, the boys (red dotted figures) leave their parents' house to live in that of their mother's brother, as indicated by red arrows. When of age, the older boy marries the oldest daughter of the house (green figure). In turn, the younger boy weds the daughter of his father's sister (blue dotted figure). Since kinship follows the mother's line, the boys belong to the Wolf moiety, the girls to the Raven.

and heavily laden canoes bring chests filled with dried salmon and fish oil, blankets and fur robes, handsomely carved war clubs and bowls. Watching this bustle of activity, the little boys of the villages collect shells, whittled sticks and perhaps a rabbit-skin or two and give play potlatches of their own.

When the day of the potlatch arrives, the distinguished guests appear dressed in their finest, most ornate garments. Some wear richly fringed blankets completely covered with intricate, colourful designs representing animals, birds and sea creatures; others have draped their shoulders with robes of sea otter, marmot or black bearskin. About the necks of many hang strands of tusk-shaped dentalia shells. The guests have travelled from their villages in mighty ceremonial dugouts, some more than 50 feet long, with high and elaborately carved and painted prows and sterns. Landing at the shore in front of their host's new house, they are greeted by minor members of his community, who give them food and capes and conical hats of woven cedar-bark fibre to keep off the drizzle that has set in.

At midday, the host himself and his wife emerge. They are splendid figures. The chief is draped in a fringed blanket that his wife has woven to his personal design; on it is an eagle, depicted as though the animal had been split lengthways so that its two halves, joined along the back, appear in profile (*page 69*). On his head is an elaborate headdress bearing a carved human face with abalone-shell eyes and heavily fringed with ermine tails. His wife is less ornately but still richly dressed in a robe of mink skins bordered with marten. The guests march up from the shore, past the still-to-be-erected portal pole and towards the deep pit dug in front of the house to receive

it. The chief welcomes them in traditional phrases, then gestures to his younger brother who gives the sign for the pole-raising. With a yell, all the chief's relatives surge forward, seize the massive pole and hoist it into position. Then, as some steady it with props, others scoop earth into the pit around the base, tamping it down firmly with sections of log.

With the pole solidly set, the host signals his guests to pass through the doorway piercing its base and into the house, where blankets and mats have been placed around the central fire pit. The wooden racks that normally store smoked salmon overhead have been removed, and the rafters are hung with the fancy blankets and rich fur robes that the host will give away; on the floor below are piles of other valuables, including dishes and bowls of elaborately carved wood, necklaces of dentalia shells, wooden helmets, armour of hardwood slats sewn together, and boxes and baskets filled to overflowing with dried salmon, seeds, seaweed and other delicacies.

But before this wealth is distributed, there is a feast. The women bring in trays of rich and rare foods: smoked salmon accompanied by bowls of a seal-fat dip; fowl and fresh-water fish roasted on sticks; haunches of venison and bear; bowls of berries—some fresh, some preserved in rancid candlefish oil; octopus and halibut boiled in wooden boxes; and as a special delicacy, well-rotted salmon roe and halibut heads. Though the guests, out of courtesy, stuff down every morsel they can hold, there is far more than even the greediest can consume; the remainder will be given to them to take home.

As the enormous meal ends amid a chorus of polite belches, the host climbs heavily to his feet. In a singsong tone he recites his names and titles, the great deeds of his ancestors and his own achievements as a mighty hunter, warrior and potlatcher. At a sign, a slave pours a boxful of candlefish oil on the fire as the host explains that he fears his guests may be getting chilly. As the fire flares up, the nearer guests must shift their seats lest they be singed, and the potlatch-giver takes great satisfaction in the subtle way he has forced other chiefs to move back, thereby enhancing his own prestige.

Finally come the gifts, presented according to the recipient's rank. Most valuable of all are blankets of cedar-bark fibre interwoven with threads of soft mountain-goat wool, some in natural white, others dyed black, blue or yellow, to create geometric patterns or conventionalized animal designs. Each blanket has taken a woman months to make. Several of the choicest blankets are handed to the highest-ranking guest, together with four robes of sea-otter pelts, ten of marten fur and seven of bearskin; the lesser guests divide among them the remaining blan-

kets, 35 robes of mink and 50 of deerskin. The chief's brother checks the gift-giving process, making sure that the presents handed out to each man correspond to his rank; a mistake would be considered a serious social blunder, to be atoned for only by another, face-saving, potlatch.

For two or three days longer the potlatch goes on, with more feasting interspersed with religious ceremonies, dances and gift-giving until the piles of presents are gone. Next year, or the year after, it will be repeated by one of the attending guests or by the chief of some other community down the coast.

The luxurious life of the Northwest Indians survived almost into the 20th Century—some of their customs were recorded in photographs (*pages 77-87*). In other parts of America, such as the desert, foraging continued. But elsewhere—long before Europeans arrived—many ancient Americans had turned to farming to sustain larger populations, more settled communities and increasingly complex societies.

The Good Life in the Northwest

The original affluent Americans were the Indians who lived in the lush coastal strip stretching from California to Alaska. Prospering by foraging, the Indians became truly rich off nature's bounty. This easy way of life lasted into the early 20th Century, when these photographs were made.

Wealth brought to the region's 100-odd tribes both blessings and curses. It allowed the Indians to settle and enjoy leisure. They had time to ponder the spirits and invent elaborate rites to honour them, to amass and decorate objects, transforming them into high art. But wealth also led to rigid social stratification, ostentation and, eventually, to deliberate wastefulness.

A Kwakiutl wedding party, photographed around 1900, is ferried to shore in a canoe with a carved and painted eagle figurehead.

Living off the Riches of the Waters

On the shore of Graham Island, off the coast of British Columbia, the houses, totem poles and canoes of Haida villagers face the principal source of their riches: the water. The Haida, known as the most skilful of Coast sculptors, continued until the late 19th Century to erect the towering totem poles before their houses—a custom derived from the ancient tradition of framing their doorways with massive wooden posts carved with figures.

Ocean and teeming river waters were the essential sources of wealth to the Northwest Coast Indians, and they knew how to exploit them to their fullest. They supplemented foraging by hunting big sea mammals; the Nootka of Vancouver Island, British Columbia, and their Makah neighbours to the south on Cape Flattery became specialized whalers as skilful as the Eskimos farther north.

The Wishram, Kwakiutl and Haida, like most Northwest tribes, thrived equally well by gathering game less challenging than whales or seals. Marine life in many other forms—small mammals, shellfish, giant halibut and sturgeon—was plentiful, and the most abundant of all was salmon. Fighting currents to swim upriver at regular intervals and spawn in the fresh-water streams and lakes inland where they had originally hatched, the salmon seemed to ask to be picked out of the water; they could be harvested with nets and spears, or occasionally just with a quick hand.

A Makah whaler hefts a harpoon equipped with sealskin floats.

Using a dip net, a Wishram gathers salmon swimming upstream.

A Potlatch: Noblesse Oblige

A Tlingit chief displays his everyday finery: a necklace of grizzly bear claws, a crown of polished mountain goat horns topped with puffs of down, a ring through his septum and traditional face paint. For a potlatch, he would have been still more elaborately clad.

Outfitted in their most sumptuous garb, high-born guests gather for a potlatch. In the foreground, two Tlingit chiefs from neighbouring villages perform a rite over a killer whale effigy before the expansive gift-giving begins. Their headgear is carved with the images of birds. On top of the carvings, stacked cylinders of woven spruce roots indicate the number of potlatches each of these rich men has hosted: the chief at right, two; the one at left, seven.

Although every able-bodied member of a tribe participated in the gathering of wealth, the primary owners of goods were the chiefs and noblemen. But these aristocrats were obliged to give away some of their riches in a potlatch. (The word is derived from a form of the verb "to give" used by many of the tribes.)

When a chief held a potlatch, he handed out much—or even all—of his wealth to his guests, confident that he would be repaid as a guest at a later potlatch. One aim of such prodigal partying was to influence important neighbours: the recipients took the opportunity to evaluate him. He had to demonstrate inexhaustible wealth and generosity by distributing food and goods. If, unlike the potlatch pictured below, the event proved a fizzle—the presents too few and the feast skimpy —the host's position became precarious; on the other hand, a truly spectacular potlatch assured him of the loyalty of his people and of the support of neighbouring chiefs.

Pleasing Powerful Spirits of Animals

Aware of the blessings nature lavished on them, the Northwest Indians developed spiritual practices to ensure continued riches. Animals, the Indians held, lived expressly to nourish man; yet every animal possessed an immortal, wilful spirit that could interrupt the supply of riches and bring sickness or death. Hence, religious practice often took the form of honouring, flattering and generally keeping in the good graces of the animal kingdom.

Whale hunters established spiritual contact with their prey by a regimen of baths, incantations, fasting, sexual abstinence and contemplation in a special shrine (*right*). Salmon fishermen, too, felt obliged to woo the fish. When the salmon began their spawning runs, it was thought that they were sacrificing themselves for the benefit of man. As thanks for this act, the first catch was regaled with laudatory speeches and treated like a guest at a potlatch. The bones of subsequent catches, once stripped clean of flesh, were returned to the sea, where, it was believed, they rematerialized as fish.

A ceremonial structure of the Nootka, dedicated to the sacred purpose of spiritual communication with whales, is built of planks. Carved effigies and the skulls of dead men were placed about the hut to call to the souls of the animals and urge them not to be elusive but to co-operate with the hunters.

A young Nootka whaler, draped in a blanket woven of cedar bark fibres, begins a long, trying prehunt ritual of contemplation. He is already a veteran of such ordeals of self-discipline, having only recently graduated to adult status through a rite that involved days of fasting, underwater endurance tests and lonely vigils, awaiting the appearance of portentous spirits.

A Kwakiutl ceremony initiating a chief's son into a secret society is a meticulously staged horror show. Its characters represent costumed monsters, including birds with huge, hinged bills that open to reveal fearful masks inside. The participants dance to a rhythmic din of rattles, whistles and disguised voices. Until recently, these exotic rituals were performed during winter months, when the spirits were thought to be close and thus easier to communicate with.

Chapter Four: Conquerors of the Far North

The hunter is hungry. For the Eskimos of his village on the north coast of Alaska it has been a difficult autumn and a hard winter. Early gales in the autumn had driven the caribou south before their time. Then, in the sunless winter months, almost constant storms curtailed seal hunting. Now, in February, the village has been driven to unearth one of its few remaining caches of meat and blubber, stored since last summer in pits hacked into the ever-frozen soil. Even so, times are not quite as desperate as they had been five winters back, when the hunter and his wife, barely able to feed themselves and their two young sons, had no choice but to throw away a newborn baby, leaving it in the snow to perish.

But at last the storms have let up, and the hunter and his companions are hiking out to the sea ice, where each will go his own way in search of seals. The village shaman, after chanting invocations to the spirits that guide the seal, has foreseen good hunting.

It is midday, and the returning sun, though close to the horizon, has been up for two hours. The temperature hovers around 35°C. below zero, and the hunter is dressed accordingly. Over underclothing of feathered eider-duck skins he wears a snug suit —pants and parka—of caribou hide with the fur turned inwards, and over this a longer, looser suit with the hair turned outwards; the space between the suits provides extra insulation from the biting cold. The hood of the outer suit is edged with wolverine fur

Clad in a caribou skin parka with the fur side turned in for warmth, an Eskimo from eastern Alaska displays the almond-shaped eyes that link him to Asia. This Mongoloid trait, prominent among modern Eskimos but lacking in Indians, suggests that the ancestral Eskimos reached the New World after this characteristic feature evolved in the Orient.

—the only kind that does not frost up from the moisture of breath. His hide boots are also double and lined with moss to help keep their insides dry. Beneath his outer parka he carries a pouch of boiled seal meat mixed with fat, and an extra mitten containing melted snow for drinking—he will not pick up snow to melt on the spot because the melting will take up body heat he cannot afford to lose. Behind him he drags his hunting gear on a sledge made of bits of driftwood—he has never seen a tree—lashed together and with runners shod with ivory.

Though he has been travelling for several hours, the hunter has progressed only a few miles from the village. The ice is rough at best, heaped up by shifting winds and currents into tumbled ridges over which the sledge must be laboriously dragged. At last he reaches a fairly smooth stretch and begins to look about carefully, searching for a small hump on the ice—frost deposited from the seal's breath on top of a breathing hole, where the seagoing mammal comes for the gulp of air it must have every 15 minutes or so. The hunter gets out his ice pick, a stout flint blade mounted in an antler handle, and enlarges the hole; then he skims off the ice chips with a small, raw-hide dip net lest the hole freeze over again. Next, he bores four small holes around the breathing hole and lowers into it a tough net of thin whalebone strips topped with "clinkers," or rattles, of ivory. He attaches the four corners of the net through the small holes he has bored in the ice, and lets the net sag in the water under the breathing hole. The net edges hang far enough beneath the ice so that an approaching seal will be able to swim over them to reach the breathing hole; once the animal has gulped a new supply of air it will dive down—only to become entangled

Eskimo seal hunters, like this one settling down for a cold wait at a breathing hole, use ingeniously designed gear believed little different from the equipment developed by their ancestors long ago. Clockwise from left are two knives, one of wood, the other of bone, with which to hack out a windbreak wall and seat; a harness for dragging the prey away, with a wooden "paw" for scratching a seal-luring noise on the ice; and plugs for stoppering the harpooned seal's wounds to keep the nourishing blood from oozing away.

in the net that now lies directly underneath it.

Since the seal uses several breathing holes and may not return to this particular one for some time, the hunter sets up a small hide tent in which to wait. But in the hope that the animal may be near by, he attempts to attract it by scratching gently on the ice with a pointed strip of whalebone, imitating the sound of a seal's claws on the ice. There is no immediate response, and he rolls into his tent to begin what may be a long vigil.

After several hours there is a furious rattling of the clinkers; he has caught a seal. He hauls up the net and dispatches the animal with a spear thrust; then, putting his mouth to the wound, he takes a long drink of blood—the first fresh food he has had for two months. His aching hunger eased, he plugs the wound with a whittled stopper (*page 90*)—blood is far too precious to waste—and sets the net again. Once more during the night the scene is repeated. Now, with all the meat he can haul, the hunter prepares for the long journey back. He urinates on the ivory-shod runners of his sledge to form a coating of ice on which the vehicle will slide easily when loaded, lashes his tent and catch aboard and ties over each boot a creeper—strips of ivory carved with sharp knobs to give traction on the smooth ice.

The return to the village, with several hundred pounds of seal in tow, is far more taxing than the outward trip, but the hunter does not mind. His hunting has been successful and his stomach is full; under the wavering glow of the Northern Lights he chants a song of triumph as he drags the sledge along. At sunrise, finding himself marching directly into the icy glare, he puts on snow goggles—an ivory shield shaped to cover his eyes, with narrow slits that exclude all but a small part of the light (*page 93*).

Nearing home, he sees that the other hunters, who have spread out over 20 miles of ice, have been no less fortunate; the village is busy cutting up frozen seal carcasses. An hour later, he is relaxing in his hut heated by a remarkably efficient blubber lamp—a shallow dish carved from soapstone, with a moss wick (*page 95*). Stripped to the waist, he chews a strip of raw seal liver while his wife cooks a pot of seal stew over another blubber lamp.

His hut—one of a dozen in the village—consists of a pit 10 feet square and some three feet deep covered by a dome of stones braced with whalebone and topped with an insulating layer of earth (these people know nothing of the snow-block igloo constructed by other arctic dwellers far to the east). The hut is entered by stepping down into a passageway dug lower than the hut floor, to trap cold air and keep it away from the living quarters—there is no door, but a skin can be lashed across the entry to close it tight. On one side of the passageway is a small storeroom for harpoons and other bulky equipment. Inside the hut the walls are festooned with extra clothing, hide nets containing snares for trapping small game, and tools for working flint and hide. A sleeping platform at the back of the hut, big enough for the whole family to stretch out comfortably on fox- and polar-bear skins, is only about three feet below the roof, where the warm air collects.

Once the family has stuffed itself to repletion and slept off its meal, the hunter says that he is going over to the men's clubhouse. This building is considerably larger than any family hut, but of the same basic construction. Here the adult males of the village will spend the next week eating, sleeping, repairing their hunting equipment and making new gear. At intervals, their wives will bring in food, and from time to time work will stop for a wrestling contest or an insult match, in which the men compete to see who can compose the most scurrilous songs about one another, to the uproarious delight of the listeners. These contests are only half serious; the men are hunting partners as well as friends, and most—according to custom—have exchanged wives at one time or another. Mainly, the competitions serve as a harmless way of working off grudges or relieving the tensions built up during the long, dark winter. Other amusements are quieter: telling tales of great hunters now dead or the clever exploits of Raven, the trickster spirit; and watching the shaman perform his feats of magic, such as pulling a fur mitten from an empty tambourine.

So long as the hunting remains good, the men will spend much of their leisure time over the next couple of months in the clubhouse, emerging from time to time for another expedition after seals, a trapping trip for foxes or hares or, after the spring's migrant birds have arrived, in a hunt for eggs.

By the end of April, the days are stretching out to 19 hours, and one morning a returning hunter reports that whales are moving northwards through wide cracks in the ice. Immediately the village is in an uproar. Its four owners of umiaks—light but strong, open boats made of hide stretched over a framework of lashed wood—rush to load their craft onto sleds and move out to the edge of the shore ice. Thanks to the long, sunlit days and vigorous tides, the ice has broken up to bring open leads of water within a mile or so of the village. As the boat owners chant songs, urging the whale to come and be caught, all the men pull on waterproof suits made of walrus gut.

Soon, a quarter mile offshore, they sight a spout; then two, then half a dozen. From the size and shape of the vaporous columns, they know that these whales are not puny belugas, only 18 feet or less in length, or even the larger grey whales, but the mighty bowheads—60 feet or more of meat and blubber. The boats are quickly and efficiently launched, each manned by the owner-steersman and six paddlers, plus a harpooner who sits in the bow.

As the whales dive, the paddlers in the lead umiak dig in, while the captain steers towards the area where he expects the animals to surface again. The harpooner checks his weapons: five-foot harpoon shafts with detachable ivory heads having razor-sharp stone tips, coils of walrus-hide line attached to each harpoon head, and six-foot spears ending in broad, six-inch flint blades. Suddenly, 20 feet away, an enormous black back breaks water and the whale blows with the sound of a giant's sigh. Carefully, the paddlers edge the bow of the boat in, following the harpooner's gestured directions until, less than 10 feet from the whale, he stands erect, seizes a harpoon from its ivory crotch and hurls it at the animal. As the head sinks in, the shaft falls away, to be retrieved later; for the moment the crew is totally occupied in keeping clear of the whale's thrashing. The line whizzes overboard, carrying with it drags of inflated sealskins. The whale sounds, and again the boat follows its probable underwater course. Again it emerges, and a second harpoon is flung, followed by a third, each with its sealskin drags. At last, tired by its wounds and the tug of the drags, the whale no longer sounds but rests quietly on the surface.

Now comes the most dangerous part of the whale

An Eskimo fisherwoman wears slitted goggles of ancient origin—one of many designs carved from wood or ivory (inset)—to avoid the "snow blindness" caused by the brilliant glare of an all-white environment. In some goggles the eyepieces are smeared inside with soot to help absorb light.

hunt. Cautiously, the boat is paddled up to the side of the great beast. The harpooner thrusts his spear into the whale's side, searching for a vital spot. The animal thrashes convulsively, and the boat hastily backs away from the flailing 10-foot flukes. But the frail craft quickly darts forward again, and the harpooner thrusts once more, then a third time and a fourth. At last the whale spouts, not white but crimson; the spear has struck a lung. The captain orders the paddlers to backwater quickly, lest the boat be caught in the animal's death throes.

In another 10 minutes, the whale floats dead amid the bloody foam of its last struggle, and the crew raises a long shout of triumph. Hearing it, the other boats, which have been less successful, close in to help with the slow job of towing the immense catch to shore. After three hours of steady paddling, they reach the shore ice, and everyone in the village joins in to drag the carcass, inch by inch, onto the ice where it can be butchered. First, however, the head is severed, and the wife of the victorious boat captain ceremonially offers it a drink of fresh water. "We thank you for coming," she intones; "you must be thirsty." She then urges the whale's spirit, released by the severing of the head, to return to the land of the whales and tell his fellows how well he has been treated. Without this ceremony, the people fear, the whales will not return next year.

Six weeks later, the last of the bowheads have begun to pass up the open leads into the Arctic Ocean to summer near the Pole; but by now the hunters have managed to kill no fewer than five of the monsters. The heaped tons of meat are buried in the cache pits for the coming winter. In addition, there is plenty of extra blubber that can be rendered for oil, which the hunters can exchange for furs and caribou skins when they make their summer trading expeditions to inland settlements. For their own village, the year so far has been good.

Of the many remarkable cultures that developed in ancient North America, the one described above is perhaps the most remarkable, considering the conditions under which it evolved. The re-creation of the life of Alaskan Eskimos 4,000 years ago is conjectural. But many characteristics of this way of life apparently endured with minor modifications for several thousand years, almost until the present. When these parallels are combined with the archaeological evidence, it is possible to reconstruct much of ancient life in the Far North—and even to speculate with some assurance about such intangibles as the spiritual beliefs held by the ancestral Eskimos.

The bleak land these people occupied—as their descendants still do—was the Arctic coast and the adjacent tundra, an enormous expanse reaching from the Aleutian Islands off southwestern Alaska eastwards to Greenland. All together, it constituted one of the most unpromising and demanding environments ever inhabited by man. For the Eskimos to survive in such taxing surroundings called for ingenuity and inventiveness to an extraordinary degree.

Even during summer when the sun shone around the clock, this was an inhospitable realm. Summer temperatures averaged around 10°C., enough to allow the topsoil to thaw—usually into mosquito-infested bogs. In a few places, notably northeastern Canada and Greenland, there was hardly any soil at all, since the land had been scraped down to bedrock by the ice-age glaciers. Because of the short growing sea-

An Eskimo family nestles on the raised seating and sleeping platform of their igloo as a meal of codfish and seal meat simmers in hanging dishes (right background). For light and for cooking, Eskimos burn seal oil or caribou tallow in shell-shaped soapstone lamps equipped with moss wicks. Three such carved lamps are shown in the top inset, along with a rectangular, thong-handled cooking vessel. The broad scoops in the bottom inset, carved of musk-ox horn, are used by the women for stirring and serving hot food.

son, the low summer temperatures and the intense wind, the plants were small, tough varieties—dwarf willows, lichens, mosses, sedges and low grasses. Limited though the vegetation was, it served to nourish sizeable herds of caribou and musk oxen and millions of tiny animals like the vole and lemming, which in turn supported foxes, wolves and weasels. The small lakes and uncountable ponds and pools were full of fish and attracted hordes of waterfowl.

If summer was uncomfortable but bountiful, winter was almost intolerable. In the endless midwinter darkness, temperatures *averaged* below zero, dropping at times to −45°C. Storms alternated with spells of quiet weather in which even the little heat that remained in the earth radiated away into the clear, dark skies. The birds and most of the herds moved south, and many of the remaining animals hibernated.

Who were the people who mastered such a land? Archaeological evidence from a few coastal sites in western Alaska indicates that humans lived there 5,000 or 6,000 years ago. And some ancestors of the Indians must have stayed there for varying lengths of time before drifting south, although few of their relics have been found in Alaska. What happened to these earliest inhabitants is unclear. What is clear is that the people who made a permanent home in the frigid northland are relatively recent immigrants to the New World. The Eskimos—and their relatives the Aleuts—apparently arrived on the coast and islands of western Alaska from Siberia before 2000 B.C. By then the Bering Sea land bridge had long been submerged, so they must have crossed either by boat or by walking over the pack ice, which on occasion jams the 56-mile-wide Bering Strait solidly enough to form a perilous bridge between Asia and America.

Several kinds of evidence support the idea that the Eskimos reached America fairly recently. For one thing, the oldest Eskimo artifacts are only about 4,000 years old. Moreover, the Eskimos resemble the peoples of northeast Asia much more than they do other American aborigines. Their skin is relatively light; their profiles are almost invariably flattened, with short, broad noses; and their eyes are narrowed by the fleshy lids and Mongoloid fold found in eastern Asiatic peoples. Their languages also indicate a recent link with Asia. The several Eskimo tongues and Aleut show similarities to one another and to Chukchi, Kamchadal and other languages spoken on the Asiatic side of the Bering Sea. They bear no resemblance to American Indian languages.

The way of life that began among the earliest Eskimo arrivals and ultimately spread from Alaska to Greenland was everywhere regulated by the environment. The people wore layers of fur and hide clothing because they would have frozen if they had not. The climate forced them to live, at least during the long winter, in well-insulated shelters, either pit houses or, in the central Arctic, in igloos built of snow blocks. And although they hunted some land animals year round, they lived mainly off the sea, by hunting seals, whales and other marine mammals.

Over the centuries, this basic survival pattern was elaborated with extraordinary technological ingenuity, but the explanation of how it evolved into a typically Eskimo culture must await further discoveries of arctic archaeology. One thing seems fairly evident, however; the Eskimos must have brought with them to America the fundamental inventions that enabled them to exploit northern seas. Chief among these imports was the skin boat.

An Eskimo woman scrapes bits of fat off a caribou hide. In this initial step of leather preparation, knives with metal or ground stone blades (top inset) are used. After the hide has dried, blunt-edged scrapers soften it (bottom inset); easily clasped handles with finger holes cut to the owner's own measurements make the job easier.

Piercing a piece of caribou antler to make a knife hilt, an Eskimo employs a bow drill as his early ancestors did. He steadies the drill by gripping the bone mouthpiece in his teeth and spins the shaft by pulling on the bow. Most such bows are strung with strong sealskin thongs, and many are decorated, like the one in the inset, with intricate carvings.

The regular pursuit of whales is the hallmark of the earliest Eskimos, the so-called Old Whaling people, whose relics have been discovered on Cape Krusenstern in northwest Alaska. These finds date from around 2000 B.C. The whalers had large flint blades that presumably tipped heavy-duty harpoons, and while no preserved bits of boats have turned up, Old Whaling sites have yielded plentiful deposits of whalebone, testimony to the prowess of the whalers as hunters on the open sea.

To the basic necessity of seaworthy boats, the ancient Eskimos eventually added an astonishing array of special tools and devices for just about every exigency of polar living. Their harpoons, for example, were often composed of a half-dozen parts. One widely used had a detachable walrus-ivory head fitted with a tip of flint or ground slate, in which a hole was drilled for attaching a line. The head was lashed not to the main harpoon shaft but to a flexible bone foreshaft; to give added flexibility the foreshaft was seated in an ivory socket fitted onto the main shaft—and foreshaft, socket and shaft were lashed together with hide or sinew (*page 102*). The shaft itself was further equipped with a bone or ivory thumb support for added leverage in throwing.

Eskimo ingenuity also produced one of the strangest shelters ever devised by man: a house that, although constructed entirely of snow and ice, kept living quarters above freezing while outside temperatures dropped to −40°C. The origin of the igloo is impossible to trace—when it melted, of course, it left no signs that it had even existed—but in prehistoric times it probably differed hardly at all from those still made today by Eskimos in the central Arctic. Here a man and his wife can build a family-sized igloo, nine to 15 feet in diameter, in an hour or so.

To build an igloo, the husband first draws a circle on firm snow to outline the structure; then, with a spatula-like bone or antler knife, he cuts snow inside the circle to make rectangular blocks about four inches thick. Standing within the circle, he arranges the blocks in an ascending spiral that gradually closes in to form a dome—the only type of dome, architects have pointed out, that can be constructed without scaffolding, which in the treeless northern Arctic is out of the question. For a draughtproof entry, he builds a tunnel like the one used on a pit house, but of snow blocks. Meanwhile, his wife, working outside the igloo, shovels a plastering of snow over the walls to fill any cracks or holes.

Once the shell of the building is completed, a sleeping platform and a "kitchen table" are built of snow, packed solidly within frameworks of snow blocks. To supply illumination, a window of clear ice is placed in the wall near the entrance—and outside the window a large snow block is set to reflect light inside. Heating is by a blubber lamp, which transforms the inner surface of the roof into a smooth ceiling of ice that never drips; instead, a film of meltwater flows towards the floor, where it refreezes.

Harpoons and igloos are only two examples of the Eskimos' specialized equipment. Excavations at a single north Alaskan site near Point Barrow, dating from around A.D. 500 and containing the remains of only about a half dozen pit houses, have turned up a staggering list of tools—among which are most of those mentioned in the account of Eskimo life that began this chapter. The hunting gear included spear throwers and their spears, nine kinds of bone bolas for bringing down birds and more than half a dozen dif-

ferent types of harpoon heads. Along with bows were marlinspikes to tighten bow lashings, arrow shafts and six varieties of bone arrowheads—some with multiple barbs for killing large prey. There were also mouthpieces for blowing air under the skin of a harpooned seal so that the body would not sink.

Other ancient Point Barrow Eskimos had wrenches for straightening arrow shafts, hooks for hauling blubber off a whale carcass, the gorge (a double-pointed piece of bone with a line attached to the middle; when a greedy fish gulped it down it jammed in the throat). For travelling over the snow and ice, there were sleds as well as toboggans made of whalebone strips lashed together. An abundance of boat remains—some of which were surely children's toys —showed that by this time, 1,500 years ago, the skin-covered kayak and the umiak used in whale hunting had developed into forms closely resembling their 19th Century counterparts. And in addition to this hunting and fishing equipment, the Point Barrow sites disgorged what amounted to the inventory of an ancient hardware store: antler snow-shovel blades, probes for sounding out treacherous-looking stretches of snow or ice, whetstones, engraving tools, bow-drills, whalebone digging tools, stone knives and adzes for working driftwood, needles and needlecases of bone, and dozens of other specialized tools.

It is no wonder that the excavator of the Point Barrow site, the late James A. Ford, of The American Museum of Natural History, describes the ancestral Eskimos as "gadget-burdened". Both they and their Aleut cousins had a disposition towards invention and innovation; indeed, if they had not had a tendency to seek out new ways of coping with the rigours of the Arctic, they very likely could not have settled

there in the first place. They appear to have been willing to try almost anything once to see whether it would work. In the case of the Aleuts, this pragmatic twist had, by historic times, extended beyond mechanical inventiveness to produce some striking parallels to the modern scientific method. The Aleuts in the 19th Century performed autopsies to ascertain the cause of death, and dissected sea otters to study comparative anatomy, believing that this animal possessed the structure most similar to that of man (which, among the animals known to them, it did). Moreover, if a dispute turned on child rearing, two children might be raised by different methods to see which one turned out better.

The innovative, willing-to-try-anything-once atti-

An Eskimo music-maker strikes the rim of the ancient hand drum called a tambour to provide the beat for an exchange of male raillery and scurrilous tall tales (left). Above, another tambour player accentuates dance steps in a pantomime of an amorous bear. Some tambours are works of art, painstakingly assembled and deftly decorated, like the one in the inset.

Ready for the kill, a hunter poises a five-foot-long harpoon. Two kinds of harpoons are shown in the inset at right: one has a fixed foreshaft of narwhal tusk and a knifelike head for thrusting through a seal's breathing hole in the ice; the other, hurled from afar, has a movable foreshaft, shown angled and without its head to reveal the construction. Both trail a rawhide line (bottom inset), to which an inflated animal bladder (left inset) can be attached as a float and drag.

tude of the Eskimos and Aleuts may help to explain the difficulty of tracing their development. The archaeological record contains the remains of ancient cultures that, while basically similar, produced very different styles of art and artifacts. Furthermore, some of these styles have no clear-cut relationships to either earlier or later styles in the same area—even though the objects themselves served a common purpose and are, in fact, still used by modern Eskimos.

The problem of doing research on the ancient Eskimos is compounded by the formidable obstacles diggers must overcome in the Arctic. While a number of ancient sites are within easy reach of civilization—one turned up conveniently on the campus of the University of Alaska, near Fairbanks—others lie in places remote and almost unmapped. Only fairly recently have these become easily accessible, thanks largely to helicopters. Even so, digging can be done only during the short summer and then it raises unique difficulties. After an archaeologist spades down to the eternally frozen "permafrost" layer, he must wait for each day's sun to thaw a few inches of soil for further excavation. The permafrost's natural deep-freeze has its advantages; it preserves otherwise perishable materials such as bone, antler and wood. But it also has its drawbacks; it likewise preserves prehistoric garbage and feces, which, as one archaeologist tersely remarks, "release their characteristic odours" as they thaw. Nevertheless, this refuse is a rich source of information about ancient diets, and bones from migratory birds provide clues as to what season of the year a site was occupied.

The physical, if not the aesthetic, obstacles to excavating in such permafrost country have hampered efforts to establish which people preceded which by the conventional method of digging down vertically and noting the order in which later remains overlie earlier ones. This difficulty led arctic archaeologists —notably J. Louis Giddings of Brown University—to work out a completely different way of determining prehistoric successions. At a number of places along Alaska's west coast, an observer in a plane will note a wide expanse of beach scarred by ridges and furrows and looking as if some Brobdingnagian ploughman had tilled the land. These ridges serve to mark a kind of beach calendar. They represent the crests of beaches formed successively over many centuries by the shifting offshore currents. Each beach lies parallel to the next and a little farther out from the original shore.

These beaches fascinated Giddings. At one site above the Arctic Circle near Cape Krusenstern, he mapped no fewer than 114 of them; together they formed a corrugated strip of grass, brush and bog from two to four miles wide between the sea and a shallow lagoon. He reasoned that any prehistoric people heavily dependent on the sea for their subsistence would naturally settle on the ridge of the outermost beach then in existence. This site would give them the best lookout point for seal and whale and the quickest access to the sea. It should follow, Giddings reasoned, that the farther back from the sea one moved, the older would be the beaches—and the relics they contained.

And so, in fact, it proved. The eight outermost beaches contained traces of relatively recent Eskimos, while the next 11 produced house foundations and artifacts dating from around A.D. 1000. These finds resemble others that had turned up earlier from Alaska to Greenland, relics of the Thule people, so named after a village in Greenland. The artifacts from Cape Krusenstern were similar enough to those of historic Eskimos to make clear that the latter are direct descendants of the Thule people. Still farther back, a mile from the sea, beach No. 53 yielded remains of the Old Whalers of about three thousand years earlier and the first people known to have followed an Eskimo-like life.

Year by year and ridge by ridge, Giddings and his associates continued to unearth the prehistory of Cape Krusenstern. The very earliest beaches contained fine tools known as microblades from around 3000 B.C. Their makers, called Arctic Small Tool peoples, may or may not have been Eskimo, but they seem to have handed down their tool designs to subsequent people who were undoubtedly Eskimo.

Beyond the oldest beach, on a ridge that had been above the sea since the ice ages, Giddings found tools dating from about 4000 B.C. These spear points, generally stubby and notched on either side for lashing to a shaft, differ markedly from any made by later arctic people. Far cruder tools point to an even earlier culture, as yet undated.

These and many other excavations have revealed the chronological sequence of human habitation in coastal regions of Alaska, Canada and Greenland. What they have failed to do, however, is to demonstrate exactly how the succession of peoples of one place relates to those somewhere else—or even, in some cases, how the successive inhabitants of a single locality are related to one another. On Cape Krusenstern's beaches, a people notable for the crudity of their tools are almost directly followed by the relics of an amazingly artistic group called the Ipiutak, who flourished here and elsewhere in western

An Eskimo lashes a harpooned caribou (left, above) to his kayak. The kayak, covered tautly by sealskin, is a sleek vessel (left) whose unity of design extends to the hunter: his sealskin slicker (above) fastens around the hatch by a drawstring. This keeps the craft watertight—and buoyant, should it tip over.

Alaska in the early centuries of the Christian Era.

The richest store of Ipiutak remains has been found about a hundred miles from Cape Krusenstern, at a settlement on Point Hope. The Ipiutak people produced intricate carvings of bone and ivory—figures of men, animals and fantastic beasts, in addition to delicate chains whose interlocking links are ingeniously whittled from a single piece—and they also elaborately decorated their harpoon heads, knife handles and many other utilitarian objects. Some of the most bizarre examples of the Ipiutaks' carvings come from graves in which the faces of the dead were furnished with staring artificial eyes of ivory as well as ivory nose plugs and mouth coverings.

Perhaps the most remarkable find at Cape Hope is evidence of no fewer than 600 pit houses, the largest prehistoric community ever found in the Arctic—indeed, bigger than all but a handful of ancient settlements found anywhere in North America. But successful though the Ipiutaks must have been, judging from the size of this settlement and the artifacts it contained, the people apparently had no clearly identifiable cultural descendants; their successors at Point Hope and elsewhere left simpler material remains that indicate a higher regard for unadorned practicality than for artistry.

Given such archaeological puzzles, any overall account of Eskimo prehistory is bound to be sketchy. What is certain is that after 1000 B.C. the pre-Eskimo Small Tool people managed to spread across the top of the world: along the low coastal plain of northern Alaska and northwest Canada, through the winding, ice-choked sounds and channels of the Canadian Archipelago, and on to the foggy rocks of Hudson Bay, Baffin Island and Greenland. They even made their

After trapping salmon trout in a stone weir built across a narrows (above left), Eskimos spear the wriggling fish (above) with long-handled, three-pronged spears called leisters (top inset). Salmon are an important source of food and even their skins have a function—dried whole and cinched at the top, they make serviceable pouches for fishing gear (left inset).

An archer takes aim with bow and bone-tipped arrow (below).
This weapon (right inset) is one of many the Eskimos devised.
A simple but cunning contrivance is wolf bait (bottom
inset), a barb of whalebone, folded tight and tied with sinew,
then stuck in a hunk of fat. When a wolf gobbles the fat,
it swallows the barb, which opens in the stomach and causes
the animal to bleed to death. The knife with sheath (left
inset) is the hunter's basic personal tool, used for skinning.

way to the appallingly bleak coasts of Independence Fjord in northeast Greenland—less than 600 miles from the North Pole.

By this time the first people who are clearly Eskimos, the Old Whalers, had arrived in Alaska. They, too, spread to the east. And by around 500 B.C. they and the Small Tool people together seem to have contributed influences to the development of a distinctive people known as the Dorsets (after Cape Dorset on Baffin Island, where their culture was first discovered). The Dorsets, who are known to have reached northern Newfoundland by 500 B.C., may have been the first native Americans to have any contact with Europeans—and thus the first to cross the line dividing prehistory from history. The Europeans were, of course, Vikings, a group of them, led by one Thorfinn Karlsefni, attempted to settle "Vineland"—almost certainly Newfoundland—about A.D. 1005. There they encountered a people they referred to as Skraelings, apparently a derisive term for natives in Old Norse.

If the saga accounts of the Karlsefni expedition can be believed, the Skraelings were almost certainly Eskimos. They are described as having arrived in skin boats—which are an Eskimo innovation; eastern Indians used either dugouts or bark canoes. Even more significant, they are said to have had "remarkable eyes and broad cheeks". While Indians as well as Eskimos have broad cheeks, there is nothing particularly remarkable about most Indians' eyes. The Eskimos' Oriental-looking eyes, on the other hand, would have seemed strange indeed to most 11th Century Europeans.

Relations between the Dorsets and the Vikings were at first guardedly friendly, but eventually the two groups got into a fight. (One detail of the skirmish provides additional evidence that the Skraelings were Eskimos; they hurled poles to which were attached "large, ball-shaped objects nearly the size of a sheep's belly"—possibly harpoons with their characteristic sealskin floats attached.) The confrontation seems to have been a standoff, although the fighting helped convince Karlsefni and his friends that Vineland was not a good place to settle—giving the Dorsets the still further distinction of being the first, and almost the only, American natives to throw back an European invasion.

However, the Dorsets did not have long to enjoy their triumph; within a few centuries their culture was replaced or absorbed by that of the Thules, the direct ancestors of modern Eskimos, who elaborated on the sea-hunting tradition begun by the Old Whalers, and within the span of a few hundred years had fanned out from western Alaska to Greenland.

Exactly what spurred this remarkable spread is uncertain. A good possibility is a new invention—the dog sled, which the Thules possessed and the Dorsets did not. Dog sleds not only would have given Thule hunters considerably greater mobility, but also would have greatly increased the efficiency of winter hunting. Seal catches, particularly, could be handled far more expeditiously.

For whatever reason, Thules and their Eskimo descendants have inhabited the entire coast of the American Arctic since about A.D. 1000 and have even flowed back across the Bering Strait to the eastern tip of Siberia. In their chosen environment, the ancient Eskimos evolved a way of life that represents an extraordinarily successful example of ingenuity, persistence and courage under appalling difficulties.

Chapter Five: Farmers of the Southwest

Around 5,000 years ago the rise of a new skill—farming—signalled the beginning of revolutionary changes in the North American Indian way of life. The same transition had occurred earlier in other parts of the world, but nowhere had it taken place in a more unlikely region: the southwestern corner of the present United States.

The environment of the Southwest was then much as it is today. And a tourist driving through large sections of Arizona and New Mexico cannot help but be struck by the poverty of the land. Here are no lush green fields or fertile bottom lands, but stony, dry desert, hot in summer, cold in winter, swept by winds, dotted with straggly mesquite and spiny cactus—land that might support the flocks of a few poor herdsmen but that seems hardly the sort of place to inspire men to plough and sow.

Yet it must have been the very poverty of the region that influenced its inhabitants to try farming in those areas where conditions were favourable enough to allow it. There was too little vegetation to attract large herd animals, so big-game hunting was scarcely a profitable occupation. Nuts and small animals could be found, but only in quantities sufficient to support a relatively thin population. So the idea of helping food plants to grow must have had a powerful appeal when it finally reached the Southwestern Indians from Mexico.

The earliest evidence of agriculture in the New

Stylized figures, their hands clasped in ceremonial dance, decorate this detail from a thousand-year-old earthenware vessel. Made by the Hohokam Indians of southern Arizona —one of the first tribes to shift their emphasis from foraging to farming—it indicates an increased concern with ritual, brought about, like pottery, by a more settled way of life.

World comes from Mexico. By 8000 B.C. some of the American foragers had learned to domesticate some of the wild plants whose seeds had long formed a part of their diet, and were raising half a dozen crops. Among them were the three that would ultimately become staples among all farming peoples in both Central and North America: beans, squash and corn. Thus, it is not surprising that agriculture, spreading northwards, entered what is now the United States in the area closest to Mexico, the Southwest, where the inhabitants of Bat Cave in southwestern New Mexico were raising a primitive kind of corn by about 3000 B.C.

It took a long time, however, before agriculture could provide even as much as half the food supply of the Southwestern peoples, and for centuries they remained more desert foragers than farmers. The climate held them back, and so did the plants they tried to grow. The earliest corn found in Bat Cave, for example, was still only a step or two removed from its wild ancestor. That plant, now extinct, possessed cobs little more than an inch long, holding only a few dozen kernels. Moreover, its miniature ears, unlike those of modern corn, were not enclosed and protected in a tight husk, so that the grains were exposed to the competitive foraging of birds and rodents. The types of corn that followed were only a little more productive, but gradually over the centuries the Indians of the Southwest acquired improved plant strains. Meanwhile, they had to find ways to overcome the shortage of water, especially the limited amount of rainfall, which to this day makes simple dry farming, without the aid of irrigation, a singularly chancy business in much of the region.

Precipitation in most parts of the Southwest comes

mainly in summer, usually in the form of brief but intense thunderstorms whose water runs off downhill before much seeps into the ground. To make the most of the limited moisture the farmers learned to build check dams of loose stones across the small arroyos that channelled the runoff. The dams not only slowed the rush of water to increase its absorption by the ground but also trapped sediment to form little terraces of more than average fertility. In spots where a spring seeped out along the base of a cliff, a group of farmers might wall off a small area, which they would then fill with dirt and trash to make a garden. On lower ground, along the larger streams and rivers, a tribe would arrange its fields so as to take advantage of flooding from showers or from melting snow in the mountains upstream. Some people doubtless employed "pot irrigation" similar to that still used in parts of Mexico and the Southwest, carrying water to the fields in clay-caulked baskets, skin bags or pottery containers. And in a few places Southwestern Indians ultimately constructed elaborate irrigation works, storing water in reservoirs and distributing it through canals.

Farming techniques also improved, though tools never seem to have developed beyond the simple digging stick of pointed hardwood, useful alike for unearthing wild roots, for punching holes in the soil to plant seeds and for gouging out a new irrigation canal. Crops were sown in early spring when the subsoil was still moist from winter seepage. Corn was sown in deep holes and in clumps widely scattered over the plot to minimize demands on the limited water; each clump contained enough seeds to produce 10 or a dozen plants. As the stalks grew—seldom more than three or four feet high—the outer plants shielded the inner ones from the hot, dry winds of summer, so that they could flourish sufficiently to yield a few ears.

By around 300 B.C., some Southwestern farmers began to settle in villages. They lived in the valleys of the Mogollon mountain range in New Mexico and are believed to be ancestors of the modern Zuñi Indians of New Mexico and Arizona. Since there is little land suitable for even modest farming in the steep mountains and narrow valleys of the Mogollon heartland, the people continued to depend heavily on hunting and gathering to supplement their sparse crops, and their villages rarely amounted to more than about a dozen pit houses.

These dwellings were roughly circular or rectangular excavations no more than two or three feet deep, above which rose a framework made of stout posts supporting a roof of saplings laid across poles. The whole was probably covered with woven reeds and a mud plaster that would exclude all but the worst of the infrequent rainstorms, and the earth into which the house was dug would have served as effective insulation against the desert heat. In the Southwest, temperatures often go over 38°C. in summer, but only a few inches below ground level they are far less extreme. The kangaroo rat and half a dozen other species of desert animals have learned to take advantage of this fact by seeking out holes or burrows during the hottest hours of the day, and perhaps their Mogollon neighbours, noting the animals' predilection for underground siestas, may have been inspired to construct what were, in effect, burrows of their own. The pit houses would have served equally well to exclude cold, which is not as rare in the desert as one might think; thanks to the clear, dry air, 38°C. at noon can drop to near freezing at dawn, while winter cold snaps, particularly at high altitudes, can be even more biting.

To the west of the mountainous Mogollon territory, considerably more elaborate farming communities arose in the valleys of the rivers Salt and Gila in southern Arizona. Here conditions were seemingly even less propitious for agriculture, since the two watercourses flow through some of the bleakest desert in North America. But forbidding though the region appears, its soil is surprisingly rich, made so by deposits of silt laid down each spring as the rivers, swollen with rain and melted snow from mountains to the east, overflow their banks.

Around 100 B.C. a people thought to be ancestors of the Pima and Papago tribes, called by archaeologists the Hohokam (from a Pima word meaning "that which has vanished"), were practicing a crude form of what is known as flood irrigation: they built dykes and little dams to divert water from the Salt and Gila to cultivated plots located near the riverbank terraces. Soon, however, using more advanced irrigation methods—probably learned from peoples in Mexico, where irrigation had by then been practiced and refined for more than a thousand years—they were constructing ditches to carry the life-giving water farther from the rivers.

The Hohokam's first simple efforts are hard to trace today, having been largely obliterated by modern irrigation, agriculture and urban development (several Hohokam settlements lie beneath the city of Phoenix). However, Dr. Emil Haury, a professor of anthropology at the University of Arizona, suggests that the earliest ditches may have been as much as 15 feet wide, although no more than one or two feet deep. Later—presumably to minimize evaporation of precious water by reducing the surface area exposed to the atmosphere—the structures were narrowed to eight feet or so, but were cut six feet or more deep. Many were lined with clay to reduce water loss through seepage.

In a few places the Hohokam built sizable earth dams to divert the water from the riverbeds into their major canals, some of which carried water for a distance of 30 miles, with branch canals leading into fields along the way. The flow of water was controlled, as in many modern irrigation systems, by a series of head gates—movable devices for blocking and unblocking a branch channel; those built by the Hohokam are thought to have consisted of tightly woven grass mats, backed by stakes, which could be raised or lowered as required.

Such complex irrigation systems clearly required imaginative engineering, enormous amounts of labour and organized management. The ditches apparently were gouged out entirely with digging sticks, the marks of which have been found on the walls of canals uncovered by archaeologists, and the loosened earth was carried off in baskets. Once built, moreover, the canals had to be maintained: silt deposited by the muddy floodwaters of spring had to be removed periodically, while a flash flood from a summer thunderstorm could break through the side of a canal and cut gullies across fields at a lower level. In exchange for these exertions, however, the Hohokam canal system could carry water to the rich valley soil far removed from the rivers, making possible a denser population and larger communities than those of the Mogollons.

The basic Hohokam dwelling resembled the simple Mogollon pit houses, but other structures—ball courts and pyramid-like mounds—were much more elaborate. The ball courts were similar to those the Spanish conquerors found in use in Aztec Mexico —oval clay playing-floors ranging in size from a basketball court to some as large as a football field. At either end of the court was a goal—stone markers or a basin into which a rubbery ball, probably made from the coagulated juice of a desert plant called guayule, could be struck.

From Spanish eyewitness accounts of the Mexican ball games, the sport seems to have been a combination of soccer, basketball, volleyball and free-for-all. The ball could not be thrown or kicked; rather, the players struck it—and one another—with their hands, knees, elbows and what the Spanish called hinder parts, which were equipped with tough leather shields. The object of the game was to get the ball into the other side's goal, but this aim was apparently rarely achieved; when it was, the scoring player was entitled to the clothing and jewellery worn by the spectators. The result was not infrequently riot between friends of the winner on the one hand, intent on helping him collect his rightful winnings, and spectators on the other, intent on fleeing to safeguard their belongings.

The obvious inference from the Hohokam ball courts—that their constructors were strongly influenced by more advanced societies in Mexico—is even more convincingly borne out by the pyramid mounds that the Hohokam built. Made of hard-packed clay and comparatively small, they are clearly simplified versions of the enormous stone-faced platforms of Mexico, and may, like their Mexican counterparts, have been topped by temples.

Still other evidence of the Hohokam's contacts with Mexico comes from their artifacts and art motifs. For example, the serpent being attacked by a bird that appears on some Hohokam painted pottery resembles an ancient Mexican design (the serpent-and-bird motif is still seen on the Mexican flag). And polished slate mirrors and little copper bells unearthed at some Hohokam sites are almost certainly Mexican imports, since there is no evidence that the Hohokam worked metal.

The pervasive Mexican influence among the Hohokam has led some prehistorians to suggest that their communities, at least in the more developed stages between A.D. 700 and 1100, may have represented colonies of some civilized people to the south. Because of the hundreds of miles of trackless desert and tumbled mountains between the Hohokam and any of the warlike Indian empires that rose in Mexico, the Hohokam hardly could have been colonials under the direct military control of others. Possibly, however, their settlements were colonial in the sense that they were semi-independent communities set up by emigrants from Mexico, retaining trade and cultural ties to their homeland. On the other hand, the Mexican traits of the Hohokam may have filtered in —as their knowledge of irrigation probably did— through simple trade.

But whatever its relationship to Mexico, Hohokam society was no mere copy of a southern original. It possessed its own distinctive traits and skills—and one of these was unique, not only in America but in the entire world. Around A.D. 1000, several centuries before European craftsmen invented the process, a Hohokam artist devised a way to etch designs with acid. The Hohokam etched on shells, which they obtained by trade with Indians living along the Gulf of California, and the discovery a few years ago of a shell ready for etching reveals how the process was carried out. The shell, found at Snaketown, a large Hohokam site near the river Gila, still bore the protective coating of pitch that the etcher had carefully placed on the part of the design he wanted raised. Had he completed his project, he then would have immersed the shell in a bath of weak acid—probably the vinegary fermented juice of the saguaro cactus fruit—which would have slowly eaten away the unprotected surface.

But despite the Hohokam's sophisticated agriculture and crafts, their way of life never spread beyond those river valleys that were broad enough, and had water enough, to make large-scale irrigation possible. By far the most widespread of the Southwestern farmers were the Anasazi, who flourished to the north of the Hohokam and Mogollons. Their modern descendants include the Hopi, but their name was given them by archaeologists who used the Navajo for "the Old Ones".

The Old Ones were not only successful farmers; they were also ingenious builders. They were the first to raise the remarkable structures that come to mind at the mention of Indian farming in the Southwest —the apartment-like dwellings of adobe that the early Spanish explorers called pueblos, meaning "towns". The most unusual—perhaps the most spectacular settlements anywhere in the New World or in the Old—are pueblos built into natural clefts high up in the walls of steep canyons. The best known of the cliff dwellings, in Mesa Verde National Park in southwestern Colorado, are still in almost livable condition 650 years after their last inhabitants left

them by the everyday route—climbing up carved toe holds in a vertical cliff.

The Anasazi originally occupied a fairly limited area known today as the Four Corners, the point where Arizona, New Mexico, Utah and Colorado meet, but at their peak, around A.D. 1200, their villages were scattered across a considerable part of each of these states. Although there are wide, barren tracts where any sort of agriculture is impossible, much of the region over which the Anasazi eventually spread is better suited for farming than the rugged Mogollon country and requires less extensive irrigation than the desert river valleys cultivated by the Hohokam. It contains mesas and plateaux whose altitudes guarantee a relatively copious rainfall, some of which could be stored in man-made reservoirs, so that in most years farming could be carried out without the building of extensive irrigation systems. The region also contains some of the Southwest's highest mountains—the Rockies in Colorado, the Sangre de Cristo in New Mexico and the Wasatch range in Utah —with many vigorous rain-nourished streams that the Anasazi farmers used for flood irrigation in the foothills and valleys.

The earliest Anasazi settlements, dating from around the beginning of the Christian Era (about the same time that the Hohokam were starting to expand their canal system), gave little hint of accomplishments to come. They were composed of dome-shaped structures that, unlike the Mogollon and Hohokam pit houses, were built around shallow depressions in the ground. Built up of concentric layers of logs laid in a sort of rail-fence arrangement and cemented with mud mortar, they seem to have lacked one feature that even most prehistoric people (including the

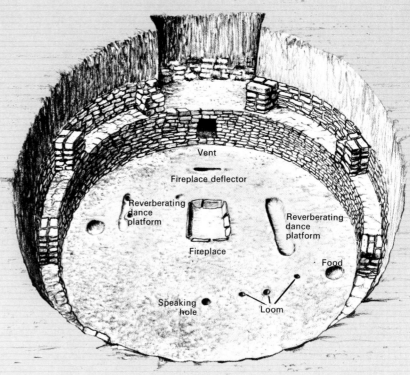

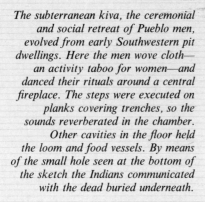

The subterranean kiva, the ceremonial and social retreat of Pueblo men, evolved from early Southwestern pit dwellings. Here the men wove cloth— an activity taboo for women—and danced their rituals around a central fireplace. The steps were executed on planks covering trenches, so the sounds reverberated in the chamber. Other cavities in the floor held the loom and food vessels. By means of the small hole seen at the bottom of the sketch the Indians communicated with the dead buried underneath.

Mogollons and Hohokam) considered essential—an interior fireplace; presumably the heating system consisted of stones warmed in an outdoor fire and then laid in a pit dug in the house floor. A possible explanation is that the log houses were covered with inflammable brush or grass, making an interior fire dangerous. Whatever the reason, the Anasazi a few centuries later were building more conventional pit houses with more conventional heating—a central fire pit, the smoke from which escaped through a hole in the roof. Perhaps to prevent sudden flare-ups caused by gusts of wind through the doorway, the fire pits were protected by deflectors—low screens made of stone slabs. Doubtless these also served to block off uncomfortable draughts in winter.

It was not until about A.D. 900 that the Anasazi began building pueblos. The origin of these singular structures is a mystery; they are unlike anything elsewhere in North America and not much like contemporary structures in Mexico. But the early Spaniards had correctly named them towns—for towns are certainly what they were. An entire village could be housed in what was, in effect, a single building. The largest pueblos were genuine apartment houses;

Pueblo Bonito, whose ruins lie in the fertile valley of New Mexico's river Chaco, was four to five stories high, contained more than 800 rooms and was arranged in an immense "D" around twin plazas. Many smaller pueblos, however, consisted of no more than a helter-skelter collection of roughly cubical modules added to at different times; they looked like something a child might make with building blocks of different sizes and shapes.

Curiously, the pit house, or something very like it, survived amid the new-style architecture, though its earthen walls had come to be lined with masonry. These circular, semiunderground chambers, entered by means of a ladder through an opening in the mud-covered roof, were the prototypes of the kivas that some Southwestern tribes still use for ceremonial purposes; probably they served the same function among the Anasazi peoples.

By the time they were building pueblos, the Anasazi had developed a culture that was vigorous enough to spread its style of architecture and other traits over much of the Southwest, apparently without warfare. It absorbed the less advanced Mogollon culture and influenced the Hohokam.

What had inspired the Anasazi to devise their widely adopted pueblos in the first place can only be guessed at. One possibility is a growing shortage of timber as their increasing population, nourished by agriculture, was compelled to build more and more dwellings. The substitution of stone and adobe for timber would almost automatically have given the pueblos their vertical walls, which imposed limitations on the shape a building could take, but at the same time would have made it easy to create an additional room by simply adding three walls to one of those of an existing structure.

An even more pressing influence than lack of timber may have been a need for physical security. The expanding population of the pueblo dwellers themselves may have caused friction between groups, leading to conflicts. Certainly many pueblos have the look of walled fortresses; on the first story, at least, doors and windows open only on the enclosed interior courtyard. The only means of entrance from the outside is by ladder—and ladders can, of course, be pulled up to leave only the blank exterior walls to confront hostile strangers.

Security seems to be the only explanation for the development of Anasazi cliff dwellings. They are among the most inaccessible homes ever inhabited. Built in regions of high mesas deeply scarred with narrow canyons, they occupy lofty ledges in the faces of sheer cliffs. Most were too high to be reached from the canyon floors, and were accessible from the mesas above them only by precipitous paths down the cliffs, some of them trails consisting of no more than a series of shallow toe holds hacked out of the rocks. A few of the dwellings can be reached today only by an experienced mountain climber lowering

himself down the cliff face on a rope. Yet the Anasazi —men and women carrying babies and bundles of food—climbed up and down several times a day between the pueblos and the croplands on the mesas above. One of the largest and most impressive pueblos, Mesa Verde's famous Cliff Palace—sheltered in an enormous cave 325 feet long and 90 feet deep, with a rocky ceiling that arches to a height of 60 feet —contains more than 200 rooms and must have accommodated several hundred people. From the cave to the mesa above lie 100 feet of vertical cliff; modern visitors with the stomach to look down while making the climb can see the canyon floor 700 feet below.

Some cliff dwellings are so well preserved that it is easy to imagine what life was like in one of them when it was a bustling and prosperous community. The time is 900 years ago. A visitor approaching across the mesa top sees no sign of a village, only cultivated fields. The fields are hardly more than garden plots of half an acre or less, scattered over a narrow strip of tableland and interspersed with a few stands of piñon and juniper, remnants of the mesa's original cover of vegetation.

It is late summer, and dotted over each field are clumps of cornstalks; between them are low bean bushes and sprawling squash vines, on which varieties of pumpkin and crookneck are ripening, as well as cotton plants that supply the cliff dwellers with material for their textiles. Around the edges of some fields are sunflowers, valued not for their blossoms but for their edible, oily seeds. The crops are almost ready for harvesting, and the fields are deserted except for a dozen boys assigned to scare off any foraging crows. The village men, who ordinarily

Nestled into the face of a sandstone cliff, Cliff Palace at Mesa Verde, Colorado, is now in ruins but once housed over 400 people in its 200 room.

e inhabitants reached their fields on the plateau about 100 feet above by climbing wooden ladders and using toe holds cut in the sandstone.

share farm work with the women—unlike most Indian men they do not consider such labour too undignified—are taking advantage of the respite to hunt mule deer in the mountains near by.

As the visitor reaches the far edge of the fields, the ground before him suddenly drops away. At his feet the tableland ends abruptly at the lip of a canyon, its nearly perpendicular walls of reddish-brown sandstone plunging 800 feet to the canyon floor. Peering over the brink the visitor still can see no trace of a village. Only the chatter of voices drifting up from below and the beginning of a narrow path leading over the canyon's lip indicate that a settlement is near by. Some 200 feet down the hazardous trail the village huddles in a large cavelike alcove beneath a rock overhang, its buildings resembling a swallow's nest under the eaves of a barn.

The village is built in a series of rising terraces. On the highest terrace, about 30 feet wide, stand houses of sandstone mortared with mud, their rear walls abutting the natural rock at the back of the cave. In front of the houses ladders protrude from a half dozen or so dark openings in the surface of the terrace —the entrances to sunken kivas. A terrace at a lower level serves as a narrow plaza, ending in a steep slope that the community uses partly as a burial ground and partly as a garbage dump—in which a flock of domesticated turkeys is foraging.

One of the village priests recognizes the visitor and greets him according to a ritual used by his 20th Century Hopi descendants: "Perhaps you came for something?" The reply is equally formal: "I came thinking of our friends." The priest thereupon invites his guest to sit and relax on the terrace before his house—actually his wife's house, into which he moved when he married her—and offers water to drink and several thin cakes, made of corn meal baked on hot stones and rolled into tight cylinders. The cakes are the village's staple food: centuries later they will be known as tacos.

From the terrace the visitor can watch the villagers at their daily activities. Since the season is warm most of them, both men and women, wear no more than a brief kilt over a loincloth, both woven of cotton grown on the mesa above. A few women, however, are dressed in loose cotton tunics, with colourfully patterned scarflike cloths over their shoulders. Many of the villagers go barefoot, but some wear simple sandals woven of rushes. Only when winter approaches will they put on more clothing —robes of deer- or rabbitskin and thick socks of woven fibre cord into which have been twisted the downy inner feathers of turkeys.

Behind the visitor, the priest's new son-in-law is adding a room to the house for himself and his bride. His principal building material is sandstone, detached by frost and seepage from another part of the canyon wall. The natural fracture lines of the sandstone produce tolerably flat blocks, though occasionally the builder employs a harder boulder to pound away a troublesome projection. He lays the blocks in courses like bricks, in a bed of mud—clay, dug from a bed at one end of the ledge, puddled into a smooth mix with water and sand, then flattened into mud pies for convenient carrying. The doorframes are constructed either of stout timbers or of longer stone slabs. When the walls are finished, roof timbers will be laid across them, then a layer of thin poles, a layer of brush and a layer of puddled clay over all. In the meanwhile, the new bride will be carrying out her traditional part of the job: flooring the dwelling with a smooth coating of packed clay.

Further along the ledge a woman is making pots. She knows nothing of the potter's wheel already in wide use in the Old World. Breaking off a chunk of prepared clay, she quickly rolls it on a stone slab into a thin coil and winds the coil in spiral fashion, forming a pot much as she would construct a basket from coils of grass. To make the base, she winds a coil into a flat, tight spiral, which she then smooths with wet fingers. Building up the walls of the pot with additional coils is a much more demanding task; if the clay is too dry the coils will not adhere properly and the sides may crack; if too damp, the walls will collapse under their own weight. From time to time the potter melds the coils together by smoothing the outside of the pot with a piece of dried gourd, and then curves the pot with her hand—gently pushing it out from the inside. Periodically she sets an uncompleted pot aside to allow its thin walls to dry enough to support the weight of more coils. Meanwhile, she begins work on other pots.

When the pots are fully shaped she will wait until they are thoroughly dry, then cover them with a "slip", a thin mixture of pure white clay applied with a piece of buckskin. When this too has dried, she will polish the pots with a smooth pebble and decorate them with a bold geometric pattern in black, using watery clay. After a final drying, the pots will be fired in a preheated stone trough over which billets of firewood have been heaped.

A group of women not far from the potter are grinding corn for the evening meal. They work at a row of bins made of upright stone slabs, each with a grinding slab slanting down from one end; using cylindrical rubbing stones, they rub the corn kernels into corn meal on the slabs, chanting the while to maintain their rhythm. Since the grinding slabs are fashioned from the same relatively soft sandstone used for house construction, the corn meal will contain a sizable proportion of grit.

As the sun drops below the rim of the canyon, members of the village who have been about their tasks elsewhere begin arriving—the boys from the fields on top of the mesa, followed by the hunting party with a deer brought down with their arrows. The priest's oldest unmarried daughter balances a large water jar upon a flattened pad set on her head and makes off for the village well—actually a clay-lined reservoir that traps the seepage of a small spring at one end of the ledge. There she will be joined by other unmarried girls fetching water and also by the older unmarried boys, who will make flattering but decorous comments on the charms of the water carriers. The custom, still common among the Hopi of the 20th Century, is a courting tradition: if one of the young men takes a particular fancy to a girl, he will ask her for a drink; if she likes him, she will give him one, and within a few weeks can expect him to ask her father for her hand.

With the approach of darkness the guest is invited into the house for dinner. Although it is the priest's home, its interior is as simple as that of any other house in the village. It consists of five roughly rectangular, low-ceilinged rooms, the largest of which, about 8 by 10 feet, is used by the family as work space and dining room. In the centre of its floor is a fire pit, whose warmth is welcome in the dry, rapidly cooling evening air, though the thick house walls still retain some of the day's heat. Into the walls, in chinks

The Apartment-House City of Pueblo Bonito

Pueblo Bonito—"beautiful town", as the Spaniards later came to call it —was the largest of the "apartment-house" communities of the Southwest. Built by the Anasazi between A.D. 900 and 1100 in New Mexico's river Chaco Valley, it was a single structure that contained 800 rooms and housed as many as 1,200 farming families, who grew corn, beans and squash in irrigated fields near by.

The pueblo was a sprawling crescent four to five stories high; it had over 30 kivas—circular, pitlike rooms where clans met. Its relentless growth seems to have exhausted the valley's timber resources, hampering further construction, and by the 12th Century droughts had apparently made farming impossible. By the time the Spaniards began their conquest of the Southwest in the 16th Century, Pueblo Bonito had long been a ruin.

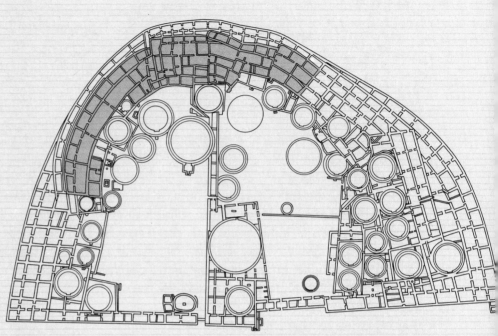

Beginning as the shaded area, Pueblo Bonito grew into a 430-foot-diameter warren of chambers

between the layers of masonry, are driven a number of wooden pegs holding bows, bundles of flint-tipped arrows, net carrying bags—some filled with edible wild roots—snares for rabbits and ground squirrels, and similar gear.

In a smaller adjoining room the family sleeps on the floor on fibre mats, each person rolled up in a blanket made of rabbitskins or yucca fibre netting thickly interwoven with turkey down. The other three cell-like rooms are for storage; ears of dried corn—the remnants of last year's crop—hang from poles near the ceilings along with chunks of dried squash strung on yucca fibre. Big jars, set into the floors or hung from wall pegs in yucca fibre harnesses, contain beans and the seeds of cultivated squash, wild pigweed and wild goosefoot.

Since there are no chairs in the house, the visitor and his host sit on the clay floor of the living room to eat. Dinner consists of gritty corn cakes and a savoury stew of turkey, rabbit and venison with beans and hominy—corn kernels steeped in a caustic solution of water and ashes to remove the tough hulls—the whole seasoned with mint, bee balm and wild onion, as well as salt obtained from the shores of a brackish lake a dozen miles from the village. Today, as a special treat in honour of the visitor, piñon nuts, toasted squash, sunflower seeds and sweetish dried squash are served; the drink is a sort of lemonade made from sumac berries, sweetened with the juice of prickly pears and served in pottery mugs attractively painted with a chessboard design.

A notable omission from the menu is fish. Though there are big trout in the small stream threading the bottom of the canyon, the villagers dare not catch, let alone eat, them. To do so would offend the rain and water spirits, whose good will, in the form of

Pueblo Bonito, built in the shape of a "D" from adobe, rose above twin plazas where public dances were held. The circular structures are ceremonial pits, or kivas, entered by ladders.

timely summer showers, is essential to the people's survival in this dry land.

After dinner the host, his son-in-law and their male guest adjourn to the kiva that functions as a combination clubhouse and chapel. There they are joined by a few neighbours who enter by way of the ladder through a hole in the roof. Around the kiva's circular walls are stone benches where some men sit while they gossip or chip arrowheads. Others sit on the floor and weave nets or baskets (a task that males traditionally perform). First, however, they formally smoke cigarettes of tobacco packed into short lengths of hollow cane; the smoke is an invitation to the clouds to release rain.

A few weeks earlier the kiva would have been reserved for a more serious purpose. Then it would have been off limits to all but the priest in charge of ceremonies, who had retired there to perform the rit-

uals required to bring on a badly needed shower —pouring water on the ground and rolling stones together to imitate thunder, reminding the rain spirits of their duty. At other times the kiva is restricted to members of one of the village's half-dozen medicine societies which, like its counterpart among the 20th Century Hopi, seeks by chants and rituals to cure villagers stricken with injury or disease. The society using the kiva carries on a sort of general practice but also specializes in the treatment of sprains and fractures; other village societies specialize in respiratory diseases, epilepsy or other ailments. Each is composed partly of priests and partly of all those who have been cured by the society—so that their membership overlaps considerably. The cured patients are expected to offer payment for their treatment in the shape of a heavy initiation fee—food, clothing or household goods.

The priest, in addition to his other religious duties, serves as Sun Priest of the village—a position of great prestige and responsibility, since it is he who must determine when crops are to be planted. In this country of high tablelands—the village is more than 6,000 feet above sea level—spring frosts are common, and if the fields are sown too soon the crop will be lost. It is the Sun Priest who, by carefully observing the increasing elevation of the sun at midday, determines when the planting season has arrived.

After an hour or so of socializing in the confinement of the kiva, the men climb out onto the terrace for a refreshing breath of air. Above their heads, between the looming canyon walls, the stars blaze out in the clear, dry air; at their feet the ledge is faintly illuminated by the flickering glow of fire-lit doorways. But the gathering chill is an encouragement for the men to turn in early, stretched out on mats beneath their fur or turkey-down blankets.

By around A.D. 1200, when the Anasazi were at their peak, the Southwest contained scores of cliff villages as well as many more pueblos that, like Pueblo Bonito in New Mexico, stood in more or less open river valleys. In all of them the life style was essentially the same, not markedly different from that observed among the pueblos of early historic times. But shortly before 1300 this way of life came to an abrupt and mysterious end in much of the Southwest. Dozens of communities of the Anasazi and other pueblo builders—all those in settled areas of Colorado and Utah and in much of northern Arizona—were abandoned. And deserted and silent they remained, unnoticed for over 600 years, until 19th Century white settlers began to discover their ruins.

Why the villages were abandoned is a mystery to this day. Since dwellings built into precipitous cliffs and pueblos without exterior doors seem to have been designed with security in mind, their desertion suggests a retreat after what may have been a period of constant attack. But nowhere is there evidence indicating widespread warfare.

A more plausible explanation is the long drought that gripped the entire Southwest for more than a generation towards the end of the 13th Century. The evidence for the long dry spell is unmistakable, recorded in the diminution of annual growth visible in the rings in the trunks of ancient trees. This climate change may have forced a migration to other areas of the Southwest with more water—principally the Rio Grande Valley in New Mexico, where 16th Century Spanish explorers found many flourishing pueblos. But drought alone does not seem to be the answer, since the settlements were never reoccupied after the drought passed. Perhaps the pueblo people did make an attempt to return to their former villages, but found the land had been occupied by other Indian settlers too formidable to be driven out.

In that case, who were these new people? Some of them may have been such desert foragers as the Utes, who had long lived in the Great Basin on the outskirts of the pueblo country and are known to have infiltrated southern Utah, Colorado and New Mexico between six and eight centuries ago. More likely candidates seem to be tribes of hunters originating far to the north—Athabascan Indians, the ancestors of the Navajo and Apache. These tribes are unrelated to their southwestern neighbours; language comparisons suggest they are connected to some of the tribes found today in the interior of Alaska and northwestern Canada. For reasons still unknown and by a route still unmapped, these northern hunting people began to drift into the Southwest during the 12th Century and had completed their takeover of the western desert by about A.D. 1500.

Certainly the migrating Athabascans would have been formidable foes. They possessed a new weapon, possibly acquired from the Eskimos—a bow backed and strengthened by springy sinew, which enabled them to shoot harder and farther than could the pueblo peoples with their unreinforced wooden bows. Most of the Athabascans picked up—if indeed they did not already possess—the rudiments of agriculture, which enabled them to support a more numerous population than any desert foraging tribe. More important, the Navajo and Apache, unlike the generally pacific pueblo peoples, were enthusiastic and skilful warriors—as the Spanish, Mexican and United States governments would successively discover during their conflicts with such chieftains as Cochise and Geronimo. Even today, Zuñi mothers frighten naughty children by telling them that a Navajo will come and get them.

In early America west of the Rockies, agriculture never spread beyond the Southwest. In most of the Great Basin, dry farming was impossible and irrigation difficult, at best, though a few desert tribes are known to have employed crude irrigation techniques to encourage the growth of some wild plants whose seeds they gathered. In most of California, dry farming was hardly more practicable, since summers were almost as dry as in the desert, while the region's food staple, the acorn, did not lend itself to cultivation. In any case, foraging was so easy in California that there was no need for agriculture. Incentives were even less pressing along the richly endowed Northwest Coast. East of the Rockies, however, agriculture spread widely, ultimately producing societies that in size and sophistication stand comparison with contemporaneous cultures in the Old World.

Chapter Six: The Mound Builders

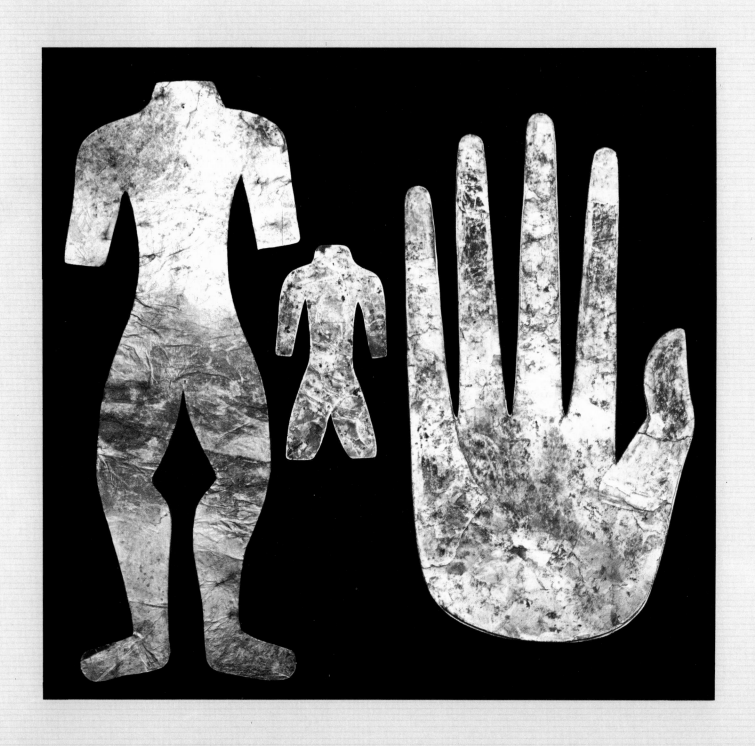

Towards the end of the 18th Century, when trappers, missionaries and settlers began pushing across the Alleghenies into the Midwest, they found the new lands dotted with hundreds of mysterious earthworks. Some were simple conical mounds, ranging from a few yards to several dozen feet high, that seemed to be graves. Others were long ridges whose outlines traced the shapes of gigantic birds or men or writhing serpents; still others appeared to form enclosures, or loomed above the countryside as steep, flat-topped pyramids.

As settlements expanded, it became apparent that the mounds numbered not hundreds but thousands—10,000 in the Ohio Valley alone. They were found in the north from western New York to Nebraska, along the Gulf Coast from Florida to eastern Texas and almost everywhere in between—even lapping over the Appalachians into Virginia. Some were of extraordinary size: one near St. Louis was 100 feet high and covered 15 acres, and elsewhere great embankments enclosed areas up to 200 acres—over 100 modern city blocks—and avenues several miles long.

Who had built these remarkable structures? The Indians encountered by early explorers disclaimed knowledge of them. Moreover, trees growing in some mounds proved to be hundreds of years old, showing that whatever lay beneath had been undisturbed for centuries. Thereupon was born the myth of the Mound Builders—a mysterious race that had reared

Cut from transparent mica with razor-sharp flint tools, these delicate silhouettes were buried with an Indian some 1,500 years ago in Ohio—400 miles from the nearest source of mica. Fragile mica was only one of many commodities traded over long distances by the Indians known as the Mound Builders; it was apparently used to decorate their ceremonial costumes.

a civilization in the American wilderness, only to be overthrown and exterminated by the Indians. The romantic poet William Cullen Bryant summed up this fantasy quite well in "The Prairies," published in 1832. Surveying the "mighty mounds," he declared:

A race, that long has passed away,
Built them;—a disciplined and populous race. . . .
These ample fields
Nourished their harvests, here their herds were fed,
When haply by their stalls the bison lowed,
And bowed his manèd shoulder to the yoke.

But then

The red man came—
The roaming hunter tribes, warlike and fierce,
And the mound-builders vanished from the earth.

However, even before the rise and spread of the Mound Builders myth, there were some who recognized the creators of the earthworks for what they really were. Writers such as the 18th Century naturalist William Bartram, who had studied mounds during his travels in Georgia and Florida, and Thomas Jefferson, who had actually excavated a mound in Virginia, did not doubt that the mounds had been built by Indians. And as early as the 16th Century, according to a contemporary account, Hernando de Soto found that Indians of the Gulf region built "high places" for the houses of their chiefs and nobles "with the strength of their arms, piling up very large quantities of earth and stamping on it with great force until they have formed a mound from twenty-eight to forty-two feet in height."

Nevertheless, such facts and sober opinions were long overshadowed by flights of fancy that viewed the mounds as the handiwork of immigrants from such widely diverse lands as Scandinavia, the Middle East and even Malaya. It was the end of the 19th Century before the builders of the mounds were seen in their true light. By 1887, Cyrus Thomas of the Smithsonian's Bureau of Ethnology, summarizing an intensive investigation of the earthworks, could declare: "The links discovered directly connecting the Indians and mound builders are so numerous and well established that there should no longer be any hesitancy in accepting the theory that the two are one and the same people." Moreover, he continues, "a study of the works in Ohio and their contents should convince the archaeologist that they were built by several different tribes and pertain to widely different eras." That is, there was no such thing as a race or a civilization of Mound Builders, but rather a number of different peoples, stretching over a long period, who built mounds.

Reality, once it started to emerge, turned out to be as remarkable as the Mound Builders myth itself. Some of the settlements were large, sophisticated cities inhabited by traders and manufacturers who carried on a thriving commerce over much of North America. They produced a culture—urbane, rich and complex, though also cruel, bigoted and caste-ridden —that was the most highly developed Indian society in North America.

Excavations revealed that the Indian engineers who planned the structures—and raised them with

The early mound builders, known as the Adenans, left evidence of themselves—and their customs—in this 2,000-year-old, eight-inch-tall ceremonial pipe found in 1901 in Ohio. The figure is that of a dwarf, with spools in his ears and a thick neck that appears to be swollen by a goitre. The Adenans are believed to have honoured deformed people.

only human muscle power—did so for a variety of purposes. Some mounds were indeed burial places —in a few instances cemeteries holding several hundred graves as well as elaborate and macabre funerary offerings. Other earthworks were designed primarily as ramparts around fortified sites or, like the enormous effigies of birds and other creatures, seem to have been the focus of burial rituals. Traces of posts and fallen walls and roofs on top of many of the pyramid mounds showed that they had been crowned by temples and official buildings.

The amount of labour and the number of man-hours involved in raising these earthworks must have been staggering. For example, the gigantic 100-foot-high mound that spreads across 15 acres in the neighbourhood of St. Louis is estimated to contain no less than 22 million cubic feet of earth, every pound of which had to be brought in, one small basketful at a time, and carried higher and higher as the mound grew.

The most recent studies among the mounds, some just beginning in the 1970s, are shedding more—and more astonishing—light upon their builders. Some communities had populations numbering in the tens of thousands, carried on intensive agriculture and large-scale production of luxuries and necessities, and possessed complex, stratified societies with an elaborate ceremonial life. Though the Mound Builders were not as rich and populous as the Mayas and Aztecs, in the centuries just before Columbus the last of them achieved something very close to true civilization amid the forests of the Midwest.

The first of the major mound-building peoples were the Adenans, so named after an estate near Chillicothe, Ohio, where some impressive earthworks were excavated in 1901. Shortly after 600 B.C. the Adenans began erecting conical burial mounds, many of them surrounded by great ridges of piled-up earth and approached through long avenues similarly enclosed. These structures seem to have been connected with the Adenans' ceremonial life, which apparently involved a sacred bird—its image, carved in low relief on stone tablets, turns up repeatedly in Adena tombs. The carvings are highly conventionalized and the "Adena bird" could be a hawk, eagle or vulture. The last of these possibilities is more probable since some Adena skeletons seem to have been buried only after the flesh had been removed, presumably by exposing the corpses to the scavenging of vultures; this practice could have led to a veneration of the birds as spirits that presided over the dead man's passage into the next world. However, with only a trifle more imagination the Adena bird can be seen as a turkey.

Experts once thought that the Adenans were newcomers to the Ohio Valley, immigrants from Mexico. They had round heads, judging from the skulls found in the tombs, while earlier peoples of the region had long heads. And their conical burial mounds resemble some simple Mexican mounds. But there is an argument against the immigration idea, for the Adenans seem to have developed their society before they grew much corn, the basis of Mexican civilizations.

A more recent and more plausible theory argues that the Adenans could equally well have been native Midwesterners who evolved from Archaic foragers, starting their culture with farming. The Adenans' way of life depended primarily on what is sometimes called a harvesting economy, a sophisticated system of food-gathering that had developed

among foraging peoples east of the Mississippi as early as 2000 B.C. It was based on intensive exploitation of only a few of the available plants and animals —deer, fish and nuts, for example. These three foods alone, plus a modest amount of greens or berries to supply vitamin C, could support a reasonably sedentary population. There are indications that the Adenans may also have practiced rudimentary agriculture, experimenting with the cultivation of corn and various indigenous plants, such as sunflower and squash. They almost certainly ate these foodstuffs, but it is not clear whether they were produced by deliberately sowing seeds or simply by harvesting stands of plants that grew wild in favoured spots.

The end of the Adenans' dominance in the Ohio Valley, a couple of centuries before the Christian Era, is no better understood than their beginnings. They were superseded—displaced, absorbed or destroyed —by widely spread groups of Mound Builders lumped together as the Hopewellians, whose name comes from a mound-studded Ohio farm owned by a man named Hopewell. Like the Adenans, the Hopewellians may have originated within what eventually became their heartland, southern Ohio, or they may have migrated from elsewhere. Their skulls, at any rate, are long, not round like Adena skulls.

It is not so much physique that links the dispersed Hopewellians, however, as style of living. For these new Mound Builders were much wealthier and more

Relics of the Hopewellians, mound builders who flourished around the start of the Christian Era, these three painted ceramic figurines portray women in everyday activities. The woman at far left sits in the manner of the modern Sioux, with both legs tucked to one side. The figure in the middle has a child clinging to her back, and the third nurses a baby.

sophisticated than the Adenans. Not only did the Hopewellians build grander mounds and other earthworks, but their burials were much more richly furnished with personal adornments and other offerings to the dead.

The Hopewellians' economy was distinctive, too. These people were not simply food gatherers or agriculturalists, but in many instances businessmen. Their wealth came from a far-flung system of trade —and even some manufacturing—centred mainly among those who lived in the valley of the river Scioto in southern Ohio. A certain amount of trade had, to be sure, been going on for centuries among the eastern tribes: copper from Isle Royale and the Keweenaw Peninsula in Lake Superior had been moving through the Midwest since about 3000 B.C., when Indians around the lake hammered tools from naturally occurring nuggets of copper metal, and marine shells valued for beads and other ornaments were distributed across the continent from the southern Atlantic and Gulf Coasts. But this trade was very informal, valued objects being passed from tribe to tribe over a period of months or years. The Scioto Hopewellians, by contrast, seem to have been systematic and at least semiprofessional traders—the first in the East, perhaps the first north of Mexico.

The Sciotans' geographical situation was peculiarly suited to commerce. To their north, over easy portages, lay the Sandusky and Maumee river systems, giving access to Lake Erie and thence, via Lake Huron, to the copper-mining tribes of Lake Superior. East of Lake Erie lay Lake Ontario, providing routes to the St. Lawrence, Mohawk and Hudson Valleys. South down the Scioto was the river Ohio, whose tributaries such as the Kanawha and Big Sandy led up into the Appalachians where mica was found. Southwest down the Ohio was the Mississippi, along which shells moved north from the Gulf of Mexico. Farther west, up the Missouri, lay the Rockies, which contributed grizzly-bear teeth for ornaments and perhaps the obsidian used by the Sciotans for keen knives and spearheads.

Scioto territory itself supplied a distinctive variety of flint; dug from a huge deposit known today as Flint Ridge, it has turned up as finished tools as far away as the Eastern Seaboard. Another local product, a fine-grained stone used for making pipes, along with some finished pipes of Sciotan workmanship, has been found as far west as Iowa and as far east as New York. The pipes, together with tools of Flint Ridge flint, indicate that at least some Sciotans fabricated articles for the export trade. Possibly the Sciotans also exported, and even raised, tobacco to smoke in the pipes they made. In early historic times, certainly, at least one tribe, in Ontario, specialized in tobacco culture so successfully that its people were known as the Tobacco Indians, while tribes in the upper Michigan copper area raised no tobacco, but obtained it by trade.

Sciotan traders did not necessarily have to travel as far as Lake Superior or the Gulf or the Rockies. Articles from these areas doubtless were still passed from tribe to tribe along a network of commercial routes—at whose centre lay the Sciotans. It is likely, however, that Sciotan traders did not simply wait for customers to come to them but actively went out after business to tribes or smaller trading centres as far as several hundred miles away. The rich evidence that has turned up in and around their mounds and other earthworks makes it easy to imagine the course

and activities of a Sciotan trading expedition setting out from a settlement near what one day would be Chillicothe, Ohio.

The traders probably departed in early autumn, when baskets full of sunflower, goosefoot, marsh elder and amaranth seeds, harvested on the flats along the river Scioto, were already cached in storage pits scattered among the village houses. They travelled in dugout canoes, perhaps five or six of them, made of oak logs split with antler wedges and hollowed out with fire and stone gouges. The largest, some 25 feet long and 4 feet wide, required a crew of six paddlers plus a captain—usually the head trader of the expedition, who might also be the supreme chief of the settlement. The paddlers were young men of modest rank who served partly out of customary obedience to their chief, partly for the gifts they received for their services and partly for love of adventure. Aside from copper bracelets, ornamental collars and breastplates worn by the highest-ranking canoe captains, the traders wore the standard Sciotan garb: breechcloths woven of wild vegetable fibre and decorated in a technique resembling batik; for an autumn trip, however, they probably carried fur capes to be prepared for chilly weather. And if they followed the customs common among later Indian tribes, their faces were painted in ornate patterns that announced the rank of each man as well as the peaceful mission on which he was bound. The expedition might have carried emergency rations—a few hide sacks of roasted sunflower and goosefoot seeds—but for the most part it lived off the country.

The bulk of the cargo consisted of trade goods —perhaps sheets of mica obtained the previous year on an expedition up the river Kanawha into the highlands of the Appalachians, nodules of flint from the Flint Ridge quarries, lumps of tough pipestone, along with a dozen or so intricately carved pipes, and several dozen pounds of dried tobacco leaves, corded into bales and covered with hides as protection against the possibility of rain.

A typical voyage took the traders down to Scioto, past sandy banks set with willows, bottom lands thick with man-high canebrake, and bluffs bearing towering beech, oak, hickory, walnut and maple. Occasionally they passed other villages of their people, and greetings, jokes and friendly insults undoubtedly flew across the water. At night they stopped at one of these settlements or, if none was near by, went ashore to kill such game as presented itself—deer, usually—and to set up their camp for the night. Three days' travel brought them to the mouth of the Scioto and out onto the waters of the majestic Ohio, here nearly half a mile wide. It then required a fortnight on the river—past the Licking, the Miami, the Kentucky and a dozen smaller tributaries—before they reached the mouth of the Wabash.

A day's vigorous paddling up this river brought these traders to their goal: another trading centre, less elaborate than their own community, but the site of a sort of annual fair. Here traders and tribesmen from several hundred miles around gathered to barter whatever valuable objects they had obtained during the past year; most had already passed from hand to hand half a dozen times. A dugout from farther down the Ohio might have brought a few dozen conch shells that had made their way up the Mississippi from the Gulf. Another, perhaps, carried copper knives and spear points that had travelled a much more complicated journey: first by birchbark canoes from Lake Superior through the Mackinac Straits into Lake Michigan, into the narrower waters of Green Bay and the still narrower river Fox, then overland along the forest trail near the 20th Century city of Portage, Wisconsin, down the Wisconsin and into the Mississippi by dugout and at last up the Ohio and Wabash to the fair.

Of the six or eight tribes ordinarily represented at such a meeting place, few understood, let alone spoke, more than a word or two of any other's language, but signs did well enough in the common purpose of buying and selling. When the day's trading in goods was finished, some of the campfires might have seen a cup and pin contest, in which the players vied to see who could most quickly flip a bone pin into a conical cup made from a deer's toe bone. As a means of redistributing goods, the cup and pin contests were presumably no less effective than the daytime bartering, for the traders, like most Indians, enjoyed gambling and often wagered so heavily on the results that a run of bad luck could cost them their entire stock of goods. If, occasionally, misunderstandings and simple high spirits led to a scuffle among the younger men, it was quickly quelled by their chieftains; by long tradition, the trading ground was maintained as a place of truce, and the spirits did not look with favour on those who broke it.

In five days or so, the Sciotan expedition would have traded all its goods for shell and copper and would have been ready to start home—full of tales, suitably embroidered, of the strange things and people they had seen, and burdened by the precious goods they had acquired. The next chief who died would receive an awesome funeral.

Proof of the wealth that trade funnelled into the communities of the Sciotans is abundant in those mounds where they buried their important dead in log-lined tombs. Accompanying the burials are not only spear points and tools, but also embossed breastplates and ornaments of hammered copper, delicately chipped obsidian knives, fragile silhouettes cut out of sheet mica and conch shells engraved with designs representing men and beasts. Some Sciotan skeletons have been found covered with thousands of freshwater pearls, which had apparently decorated a ceremonial cloak or blanket.

Not all of the rich goods found at Sciotan sites reflect trade, however; some show the cultural sophistication of the traders themselves. Pipes of local stone were beautifully carved into naturalistic animal or human forms by Sciotan artisans. Sciotan pottery also shows imagination and remarkably skilled workmanship in its shapes and decorations. Instead of painting their pottery, as did the Southwestern Indians and the Central American peoples, the Sciotans obtained their designs by engraving and by providing variations in texture; often a smooth design motif would be set off by a roughened background. One de-

That the mound builders of the advanced Mississippian culture had a well-developed sense of humour is evident from these round-faced caricatures—pottery bottles made in the form of heads. About six inches tall and just as wide, they are painted with ochre and have holes in the ears through which thongs were threaded so the vessels could be hung or carried. The lines across the lips in the centre figure are intended as decorations.

sign element commonly used by Sciotan potters is a bird resembling the Adena vulture.

In addition to carved pipes and almost sculptural pots, the Sciotans and other Hopewellians produced true sculptures: little pottery figurines that show how this vanished people sat and stood and dressed. A woman, seated with her feet to one side, wearing only a midi-length skirt, suckles her baby (*page 130*); another stands impassively beneath her elaborate headdress, long hair hanging down her back in a sort of tassel, a crescent-shaped necklace around her neck and wide bands of beads (or perhaps tattooing)

around her wrists, upper arms and ankles. And a little kneeling man, clad in a breechcloth, holds a war club or possibly a hoe.

Around A.D. 500 came a falling-off of the prosperity that had marked the Hopewellians generally and the Sciotans in particular. The great earthworks were no longer built, and the funeral offerings became crude and sparse. What caused this decline is uncertain. Since there is no evidence of invaders or conflict, the most plausible explanation seems to be shift in the trade routes from which the Sciotans had prof-

ited so handsomely for centuries. New people springing up along the lower reaches of the Mississippi may have managed to corner the supply of marine shell, thereby dislocating the entire pattern of trade in which shell was a major item.

These people, called Mississippians, eventually spread over much of the watershed draining into the great river, from Louisiana to Wisconsin and from Oklahoma to Alabama and Tennessee, and by about A.D. 1200 had developed one of ancient America's most remarkable cultures. By any criterion—wealth, population, social complexity or technological and artistic sophistication—the Mississippians were the most advanced of any Indians living north of Mexico, and their vigorous societies lasted in one form or another to be witnessed by Hernando de Soto and other early European explorers.

The Mississippians, in contrast to their predecessors among the Mound Builders, were apparently influenced strongly by Mexico, possibly as the result of trading or raiding expeditions along the Gulf Coast. Not only do their mounds resemble Mexican types, but the very basis of their advanced way of life— intensive corn-beans-squash agriculture—may well have been an import. Their strains of corn were distinctly more productive than any hitherto discovered in the mound-building area and almost certainly were grown from improved seed that originated in Mexico. After A.D. 1200, Mexican influence is more

A kneeling woman from a Tennessee grave of the 13th Century shows Mississippian fashion, front and back: a headband, plaited hair and a short apron. Skinny arms like these appear in many works of this period. The holes in the figure's armpits and wrists once held thongs; those in the ears may have been decorated with feathers or earrings.

noticeable, for carvings and pottery then begin to be decorated with a feathered serpent resembling the Aztec god Quetzalcoatl.

The level of the famous southern cultures was never quite attained by the Mississippians—they failed to devise written language, one of the essential marks of true civilizations. But in many ways they came very close. Their largest settlements, such as Cahokia (whose remains are preserved at Cahokia Mounds State Park, within sight of modern East St. Louis in southern Illinois), were the hearts of city-states with populations of 20,000 or more, putting them in a class with such ancient centres of the Old World as Ur in Mesopotamia and Mohenjodaro in India.

The great flat-topped mounds on which the Mississippians set their temples also bear comparison with the gigantic pyramids raised by both the Egyptians and the civilizations of Mexico and Central America. The Mississippian structures were monumental by any standards. The largest mound at Cahokia is 100 feet high, and has a base several times larger than that of the Great Pyramid of Egypt, covering nearly 15 acres; in the Americas it is exceeded in size only by the Pyramid of the Sun near Mexico City and the great pyramid at near-by Cholula. And this monster mound is but one of some 80 still standing in the immediate vicinity, while another 40 or so have been levelled by white farmers.

Not only do populous communities and monumental mounds demonstrate the Mississippian achievement, but so does specialization of their crafts and industries. The elaboration of their pottery, stone carvings and metalwork (the latter still based on copper from metal nuggets, not from smelted ores) suggests that some products were the work of full-time craftsmen. Nor was manufacturing limited to luxury goods. One community near Cahokia mined chert (a flintlike rock) and converted it into knives and hoe blades. Another specialized in evaporating salt from the waters of near-by salt springs—a commodity in increasing demand among people whose diet was predominantly bland plant food rather than meat. Archaeologists have unearthed fragments of broad, flat clay vessels in which the brine was evaporated over open fires. Thousands of such fragments have been found, indicating a large, well-equipped refinery that mass-produced salt on a regular basis. Since not even a metropolis like Cahokia could have consumed salt on such an enormous scale, it must have been made not only for sale locally, but also for trade up and down the river to a number of other Mississippian communities.

Many large Mississippian towns seem to have been military as well as commercial centres; the city-states they controlled may have been established by bands of conquering warriors who managed to reduce the local population to serfdom. One Louisiana community was completely surrounded by a moat that was fed by the river Mississippi; Cahokia itself was well fortified by a palisade of stout posts, complete with protruding bastions from which the city's archers could fire on attackers. Such fortifications are strongly reminiscent of the earthen mounds, topped by wooden castles and surrounded by sturdy palisades, from which the Norman conquerors of England, at just about the same time, were controlling their sullen Saxon vassals.

Cahokia, which has been studied on and off for 150 years and intensively since the 1920s, was clearly the greatest of Mississippian cities. At the height of its riches and power, around A.D. 1100, it dominated an area approximately the size of New York State. It was situated on a side channel of the Mississippi (now dried up), in the midst of an urban area extending a dozen miles up and down both sides of the river. The palisade surrounding it consisted of foot-thick logs set close together and plastered over with clay. Every hundred feet or so a square bastion of similar construction projected from the palisade; each had a raised floor that enabled the defending archers to shoot down on their enemies. The gateways to the city were screened with vestibule-like curtain walls, L-shaped projections of the palisade that forced attackers to approach an entrance from the side rather than head on. The curtain walls not only slowed them down effectively but also exposed them to a withering fire from the main wall.

Within the palisade, everyday life of Cahokia centred in the marketplace, presumably located in the western part of the city near the waterfront. Here came stone hoe blades and salt from manufacturing centres 50 miles downriver, and furs, moose hides, dried meat and copper nuggets from 400 miles away in Wisconsin. Many of the wares offered in the market were the products of workshops scattered about the city, where Cahokian craftsmen turned out goods for both local consumption and export. There were not only toolmakers, hide dressers, potters and weavers but also jewellers, who hammered ornaments from imported copper, engraved designs on shells shipped from the Gulf, and manufactured beads by drilling shells with hardwood bits and fine sand. On special occasions the focus of Cahokia's life shifted from the market and busy workshops to the city's several broad plazas, the site of festivals or games of "chunk-

Hewn 500 years ago, these two pipes were spoils of treasure hunters who plundered an Oklahoma mound in 1933 and then blew it up. The leering figure at right leans over a deer; the kneeling man wears bracelets on arms and legs.

140

The quarter-mile-long Great Serpent Mound near Cincinnati is a vestige of the mysterious Adenans, earliest of the Mound Builders. They buried their dead in log-lined tombs and earthern crematory basins at the centre of effigies like this, some built in the form of eagles, bears and alligators.

ey"—a sport in which the players tossed a heavy disc-shaped stone ahead of them and then with their thrown spears tried to pinpoint the place where it would finally come to a stop.

Yet Cahokia's most striking feature was not its protecting palisade or its market and spacious plazas, but the many mounds, large and small, that rose above the city. Some of the smaller ones held storehouses for corn and other crops, while larger mounds served as platforms for the houses of the city's more important citizens. For these upper-class Cahokians, a house that was elevated on a mound was a much coveted status symbol.

The biggest, most impressive mounds served less mundane purposes. One of them, a truncated pyramid not far from the city's southwestern entrance, was the location of sacrifices and other religious rituals; a conical mound looming beside it sheltered the graves of the city's illustrious dead.

Dwarfing all was the great steep-sided mound that was Cahokia's religious and political centre. More than 1,000 feet long—almost four modern city blocks —and nearly 800 feet wide, it rose in several enormous steps. On its topmost level, 100 feet above the city, was a post-and-wattle temple with a sharply peaked roof of thatch. From this vantage point the high priest of Cahokia could keep an eye on another structure beyond the city wall but also under his jurisdiction—an immense circle of posts, more than 100 yards across, which the priesthood used as a combined calendar and solar observatory. Here, seated on a single post set near the circle's centre, a priest kept track of the shifting seasons. By noting the position of the sun relative to the surrounding posts as it rose over the bluffs half a mile east of the city, he

determined the most propitious time for Cahokian farmers to plant their crops.

On the lower terraces of the great mound were what appear to have been residences of the supreme lord of the region, and also of high-ranking officials. These homes, like the larger building above them, faced the principal plaza and the avenues leading towards the sacrificial pyramid and the burial mound —both of them structures deeply involved not only in the city's religious life but in the strangely stratified organization of Cahokian society.

The structure of Mississippian society can be pieced together from a variety of evidence. Many facts can be deduced from the remains of wood-and-wattle houses, whose sizes presumably depended on their owners' rank—they ranged from huts to buildings 30 feet square. Burial goods found in tombs also tell much about the status of the tombs' occupants. And there are eyewitness accounts of the life of Mississippians from European explorers who, although they came too late to see Cahokia in its glory, did observe the final stages of Mississippian society among the Natchez and other tribes of the lower Mississippi

Valley. The evidence of these sources combines to give a fairly detailed picture of a bizarre society in which class levels were rigidly segregated but could be crossed in certain circumstances.

At the top of the social scale stood a Great Sun who ruled his community and the region around it with absolute power. Below him was a graded aristocracy, its upper echelon consisting of his relatives, known as lesser Suns, followed by Nobles. From the lesser Suns and Nobles came the war leaders as well as the priests, who presided over ceremonies to propitiate the gods and set the dates for planting crops. Lowest-ranking of the aristocracy were the Honoured Men, including important warriors, master craftsmen and master traders.

Supporting the Great Sun and the upper classes were the commoners—the workers, farmers and ordinary warriors who made up the bulk of the population. However, most of a community's unskilled work was done by slaves, some of them prisoners of war obtained in raiding expeditions, others bought from slave dealers. The aristocrats did not deign to distinguish between slaves and commoners, referring to both as Stinkers.

The Stinkers were a severely repressed proletariat —the Great Sun's bodyguard summarily killed anyone whose words or acts displeased the ruler —but because of the upward mobility allowed for in Mississippian society they were not condemned to a hopeless existence.

Marriage provided one route up the social scale. All the upper classes, including the Great Sun himself, were required to marry Stinkers. The Stinker mate did not rise in rank because of the marriage, but the children of the marriage generally did. Rank passed mainly through the mother, so that the child of a Noble mother and her Stinker consort, for example, would automatically be a Noble, while that of a Noble father and his Stinker wife would assume the next rank below that of the higher ranking parent, becoming an Honoured Man or Woman. This rule applied even to the Great Sun; the son of the supreme ruler, being merely a Noble, could not inherit his father's exalted position. Instead, the Great Sun was succeeded on his death by the son of his highest-ranking female relative.

Marriage was not the only way to advance in social class. An Honoured Man or even a Stinker might be promoted one level for bravery in war. And special sacrifices in honour of the gods or of a notable chief also brought advancement. But the cost was high, for such sacrifices were human; the ambitious social climber had to participate in the ritual murder of a member of his own family. One of these bloody ceremonies, which were part of funeral rites, was witnessed by French explorers during the interment of a chief of the Natchez, a southern tribe of Mississippians. Since such customs are presumed to have been common among most of these Indians, and probably retained at least a fundamental similarity over many centuries, the French observations provide many details for the following re-creation of the ceremonies surrounding the death of a powerful Cahokian nobleman, supreme war chief of the city.

The great warrior has died of a battle wound, and when his servants enter the house to tend him, they find him stiff and cold. His chief attendant orders food brought in as usual, and offers it to the dead man. "Do you no longer wish to eat what we bring

A WALLED CITY IN ILLINOIS

In this reconstruction—based on archaeological finds but partly conjectural—a dead chief's funeral procession meanders through the heart of Cahokia, the city of rich trader-farmers that flourished between A.D. 900 and 1100 near East St. Louis, Illinois. The cortege moves from the 15-acre temple mound (1), passes other ceremonial mounds built in the shape of a ridge (2), a platform (3) and a series of terraces (4), then halts at the sacrificial mound (5). Here the chief's wife and retainers will be sacrificed, to be interred with the chief in the conical burial mound (6) across the way. Protected by its own palisade at top centre is the city's economic headquarters: the market area (7). Outside Cahokia's main palisade lie farmlands, four other mounds surrounding a plaza (8) and an "observatory" (9) used to determine the best times for planting crops.

you?" he asks. "Are you no longer satisfied with our services? You make no answer; surely you are dead; you have left us to go to the land of the spirits!" Throwing his head back, he raises the death cry, a hideous wolf-like howl. It is taken up by the other servants and the dead man's relatives, then leaps from house to house until the air reverberates with the city's wails of grief.

Two days later preparations for the funeral are complete. The war chief lies on his bed of state, dressed in his finest deerskin breechcloth and mantle; his face is coloured red with iron oxide and on his head is a crown of feathers. By his side are his bow and arrows, a two-foot-long war club chipped from a single block of flint and the 12 handsomely carved pipes he has received to mark his victories. On a post near by hangs a chain of woven cane made up of many links, each of which numbers an enemy he has killed. Around him sit his two wives and some 50 of his retainers, all of whom are about to play a customary but gruesome rôle in his burial.

With the arrival of the city's high priest, richly tattooed and clad in his regalia of shell beads and feathers, the funeral procession gets underway. From the dead chief's house, it slowly winds towards the plaza before the great temple mound, and as it circles the plaza each of the dead man's wives and retainers—all of them Stinkers—is joined by eight relatives, their arms and hands coloured red, who will soon elevate themselves to honoured rank by acting as executioners in an orgy of ritual murder.

In the centre of the procession is the dead man, borne on a litter and surrounded by a crowd of women mourners raising the death chant. As the litter approaches the temple mound, the corpses of several young children are cast under the feet of the litter-bearers. The children are sacrifices, strangled by their ambitious parents, who will improve their social standing by their acts.

At the foot of the great mound the procession halts, to be joined by the Great Sun, wearing his distinctive crown of white feathers tipped with small red tassels and further embellished with white seeds. Then the cortege makes its solemn way across the city to the sacrificial mound and mounts to its truncated top, where the wives and retainers who are to be sacrificed form a line with their relatives on either side of the litter. When they have seated themselves on mats, the Great Sun signals to the high priest that the ceremony may begin.

Turning to the dead man's principal wife, the priest asks her if she wishes to accompany her husband to the land of the spirits. "Yes!" she fervently declares, "because in that land we shall not die again; the weather will be always fine, we shall never be hungry, men will not make war because everyone belongs to one people." A similar question is put to the second wife and to the 50 retainers, who also anticipate their fate and give similar answers. Their relatives then renew the death chant and dance the death dance, the sacrificial victims on their mats moving their arms and bodies in time with the rhythm.

When the dance reaches its climax, each victim is given a tobacco ball to swallow as a sort of narcotic. As he lapses into unconsciousness, a cord is placed around his neck and his relatives line up beside him, four on either side, grasping the ends of the cord. The high priest raises his ceremonial staff and brings it down with a thump on the packed earth of the plaza. The executioners swiftly draw the cords tight in a grim tug of war; in a few minutes the mass sacrifice is complete.

Amid howls and lamentations, the bodies of the war chief and the dozens who followed him in death are carried to the top of the near-by burial mound and placed in graves that have already been dug there, along with the dead man's funeral offerings of pottery, ornaments and weapons. The graves are filled in, while across the city a rising column of smoke signifies that the ill-omened house in which the chief perished has been put to the torch.

The great city of Cahokia flourished for some seven centuries. Carbon-14 dating shows that it was still occupied as late as 1550, but it had been abandoned when the first French explorers passed that way a century or so later.

One theory traces the decline of Cahokia and some near-by communities to social disintegration and warfare brought about by increased populations. Unquestionably the intensive agriculture on which all Mississippian life was based would have resulted in a sharp rise in numbers—which in turn would have necessitated expansion of the cultivated area. And here may have been the problem. Once the richest river-valley lands had been thickly populated, the northerly Mississippian city-states could have expanded in only two directions. One way was into the numerous islands of long-grass prairie that existed around them, but whose compacted soil, laced with deep, tough grass roots, was impossible to cultivate without steel ploughs drawn by horses or oxen; the other was into the forests, where trees could be felled and burned to create fields for crops.

But forest soils, unlike those of the annually flooded bottom lands along the Mississippi, are thin; even with a top dressing of wood ash they can be farmed for only a few years and must then be abandoned for a generation or more. Thus the Mississippian communities would have had to push their cultivation ever farther into the forest—and ever farther from the rivers on which their trade largely depended. This change would have produced problems not only in transporting goods, but also probably in political control: collecting taxes (as the Mississippian rulers must surely have done to maintain their elaborate standard of living) may have been simple enough when their subjects were scattered along a riverbank, but not so easy if the tax-paying villages were 40 or 50 miles deep in the woods.

In addition, expansion into the woodlands would have doubtless involved conflicts with the tribes already occupying them—who, moreover, were beginning themselves to practice agriculture, making them rather more formidable in numbers than they had been as mere hunter-gatherers.

There is no mystery, however, about what destroyed the more southerly Mississippian communities. When the French trader De la Vente visited the Natchez Indians of the lower Mississippi Valley in 1704, he found them, according to their own accounts, much reduced in numbers; this fact, he opined, indicated that "God wishes that they yield their place to new peoples" —Frenchmen, no doubt. If so, God's agents in bringing about the change were not human interlopers but the exotic microbes they brought. The Indians, because of their long isolation from the Old World, had little or no immunity to European germs, so that outbreaks of smallpox, influenza or even measles could virtually exterminate an entire community.

De la Vente himself noted that thanks to smallpox the Natchez population had dropped by as much as a third in a mere six years, and similar catastrophes must have overtaken many other tribes: microbes as well as goods can travel along trade routes. A generation after De la Vente the French finished the job that the microbes had begun: in a war against the Natchez, they exterminated most of the population and dispersed the remnant.

The fate of the Natchez pretty well typified that of nearly all the aboriginal North American cultures. Simple or elaborate, rich or poor, hunters, foragers or farmers, they succumbed sooner or later to European diseases and European guns. The heirs of the first intrepid Asian pioneers who had made their way across the Beringian tundra, of the Clovis hunters who pursued the mammoth and long-horned bison, of all the tribes and cultures who for some 30,000 years had elaborated and refined their skills for surviving and thriving in the enormously varied environments of North America, became, within four centuries, "the vanishing American".

The truth of the Indians' history almost vanished with them. Only now, as new relics of their past are uncovered and old misconceptions are corrected, has it become possible to grasp the magnitude of their achievements. The Indians of pre-Columbian North America were neither subhuman brutes nor noble savages but inventive, creative and remarkably adaptable men. At the very beginning of the time of modern humans, they took over a challenging continent. They prospered everywhere, developing not one but dozens of distinctive ways of living. Some cultures quickly became surprisingly complex—rich in art, ingenious in technology, ambitious in commerce. Within the geographical limits of one land mass they demonstrated the capacity of mankind to take whatever nature provided and build a successful, ever-expanding life—the unique flexibility that made man supreme on earth.

The Europeans Meet the Indians

While a mother crouches in grief, her first-born son is readied as a sacrifice to a chief who chats casually with a French visitor.

When 16th Century explorers finally revealed to the world at large the peoples of North America, the Indians thus presented were not the affluent traders of the Mound Builders' Midwestern cities, but the relatively poor tribesmen of the islands and coasts. Among the first to be introduced to a European audience were the Saturiwa, forager-agriculturalists of Florida.

They were portrayed—not entirely accurately—by Jacques le Moyne, who was a cartographer with a 1564 French expedition. His paintings were later published in the form of the engravings that are reprinted on these pages, accompanied by information from Le Moyne's own captions.

Le Moyne probably painted his pictures from memory after his return to Europe, since his recollections seem to be coloured by European notions. He put Flemish tools and weapons in the hands of the Saturiwa, and he tried to make the Indians look like the exotic savages Europeans expected—a preconception readily fulfilled in pictures of a people who indeed wore few clothes, engaged in sacrifice (*above*) and drank strangely powerful potions.

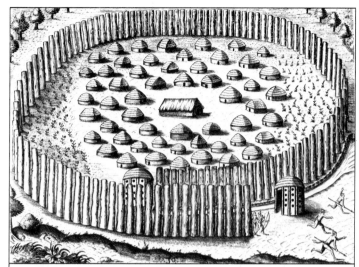

A Saturiwa village *was depicted by Le Moyne as having a log fence and guardhouse outside a narrow entrance passage. The artist also claimed that the guards were able to smell an enemy lurking near by and search him out.*

A farming scene *shows Saturiwa men hoeing with Flemish tools while at left a woman sows from a basket, European fashion. The Indians actually used hoes of large fishbones on sticks, and they carried the seeds in their hands.*

A Saturiwa medicine man *sucks blood from a gash he has made in the forehead of a patient lying on a specially constructed mat-covered log bench. After drawing the blood from the wound, he would spit it out into the gourds at his feet. Pregnant or nursing women then drank the blood in the belief that it would make their babies stronger and more vivacious. Le Moyne painted another treatment in which the patient lay on his belly on the log bench with his face over a pile of smouldering seeds, inhaling smoke that was supposed to purge from his body the source of the illness.*

Gold-seeking Indians, *knee-deep in a stream, gather sand in long reeds to sift for gold in a picture based on hearsay. Gold was certainly used by the natives, but this gold-mining method was never actually witnessed by Europeans.*

To kill an alligator, *a band of hunters forces a long pole down its throat so that it can be flipped over, exposing its soft underbelly to attack. In the background an overturned alligator falls prey to Indians with weapons.*

Disguised as deer, *Indian hunters creep up on their prey as the deer prepare to drink from a small stream. The men wore the skins—complete with antlers —draped over their backs and heads, and looked out through the eyeholes.*

Game laid out *on a wooden grating is dried by fire and cured by smoke to preserve it for winter use. The artist shows the animals lying whole on the special grate, but the Indians usually butchered their meat before curing it.*

During a tribal council, *an adviser blesses council members seated on either side of the chief (top centre). Members of the French expedition stand by holding their muskets, while women heat cauldrons of casina, a caffeine-containing drink brewed from holly leaves. The casina, served in conch shells, was so strong that, as Le Moyne shows, it caused some men to vomit (top left and right). The powerful potion was valued not only for the lift it gave, but because it also staved off hunger and thirst.*

Paddling home *from near-by islands in a dugout canoe, Indians bring foodstuffs to a public storage house like the one seen on the bank. To keep the food cool, these caches were situated in shady locations and thatched with palm fronds. The food was then taken as required by each tribesman. The Europeans marvelled that no one cheated by hoarding.*

An executioner *raises his club over two kneeling sentinels to put them to death. Their crime had been to fall asleep at their posts and allow a marauding band to burn their village.*

A chief and his bride *watch ceremonies marking the marriage from thrones on a log dais. The bride is the tallest, most beautiful of the daughters of his councillors, who flank the dais during the ceremony. Young girls, their hair tied back, execute a circle dance in which they sing the praises of the couple. Their only garment is a ceremonial girdle from which hang a pouch and a circlet of dangling copper, stone and shell ornaments that tinkle with every movement.*

Firing flaming arrows, *a war party launches a surprise attack on a village. The palm-frond huts, dried crisp by the Florida sun, ignite easily from the burning moss on the arrow tips and burn to the ground.*

R.Holata Outina.

Before a battle *an Indian chief named Outina (left) crouches next to a witch doctor summoned to give a forecast of the impending conflict. The witch doctor, kneeling on a shield within a circle of esoteric signs, works himself into a trance while the warriors and French explorers (right) look on. His body twists grotesquely as some of his bones slip out of joint, until the trance disappears. He will then tell the chief the size of the enemy force and the location of the battlefield.*

Burial of a chief *starts a ceremonial outpouring of grief that will last six months. Mourners, their hair cut short as a mark of respect, gather to lament in a circle around the grave. It is surrounded by arrows driven into the ground and topped by the ornamental shell the chief used for drinking the stimulant casina. In the left background the dead chief's houses are being burned in ritual destruction of his belongings.*

40

Welcoming spring, *the Indians make an offering to the sun: a stag skin filled out with roots and garlanded with fruit. The chief and his sorcerer, near the stag offering, lead their tribesmen in prayers asking the sun to encourage the fertility of all the plants they grow and gather. At right are French observers.*

The Emergence of Man

This chart records the progression of life on earth from its first appearance in the warm waters of the new-formed planet through the evolution of man himself; it traces his physical, social, technological and intellectual development to the Christian era. To place these advances in commonly used chronological sequences, the column at the

Geology	Archaeology	Thousand Millions of Years Ago	
Precambrian earliest era		4.5	Creation of the Earth
		4	Formation of the primordial sea
		3	First life, single-celled algae and bacteria, appears in water
		2	
		1	

Geology	Archaeology	Millions of Years Ago	
			First oxygen-breathing animals appear
		800	
			Primitive organisms develop interdependent specialized cells
		600	Shell-bearing multicelled invertebrate animals appear
Palaeozoic ancient life			Evolution of armoured fish, first animals to possess backbones
		400	Small amphibians venture on to land
			Reptiles and insects arise
			Thecodont, ancestor of dinosaurs, arises
Mesozoic middle life		200	Age of dinosaurs begins
			Birds appear
			Mammals live in shadow of dinosaurs
			Age of dinosaurs ends
		80	
			Prosimians, earliest primates, develop in trees
Cainozoic recent life		60	
		40	Monkeys and apes evolve
		20	
		10	Ramapithecus, oldest known primate with apparently man-like traits, evolves in India and Africa
		8	
		6	
		4	Australopithecus, closest primate ancestor to man, appears in Africa

Geology	Archaeology	Millions of Years Ago	
Lower Pleistocene oldest period of most recent epoch	**Lower Palaeolithic** oldest period of Old Stone Age	2	Oldest known tool fashioned by man in Africa
		1	First true man, Homo erectus, emerges in East Indies and Africa
			Homo erectus populates temperate zones

Geology	Archaeology	Thousands of Years Ago	
Middle Pleistocene middle period of most recent epoch		800	Man learns to control and use fire
		600	
		400	Large-scale, organized elephant hunts staged in Europe
			Man begins to make artificial shelters from branches
		200	
Upper Pleistocene latest period of most recent epoch	**Middle Palaeolithic** middle period of Old Stone Age		Neanderthal man emerges in Europe
		80	
		60	Ritual burials in Europe and Middle East suggest belief in afterlife
			Woolly mammoths hunted by Neanderthal in northern Europe
		40	Cave bear becomes focus of cult in Europe
	Upper Palaeolithic latest period of Old Stone Age		Cro-Magnon man arises in Europe
(Last Ice Age)			**Asian hunters cross Bering Land Bridge to populate New World**
			Oldest known written record, lunar notations on bone, made in Europe
			Man reaches Australia
			First artists decorate walls and ceilings of caves in France and Spain
		30	Figurines sculpted for nature worship
		20	Invention of needle makes sewing possible
		10	**Bison hunting begins on Great Plains of North America**
Holocene present epoch	**Mesolithic** Middle Stone Age		Bow and arrow invented in Europe
			Pottery first made in Japan

▼ Four thousand million years ago ▼ Three thousand million years ago

▲ Origin of the Earth (4,500 million) ▲ First life (3,500 million)

far left of each of the chart's four sections identifies the great geological eras into which the earth's history is divided by scientists, while the second column lists the archaeological ages of human history. The key dates in the rise of life and of man's outstanding accomplishments appear in the third column (years and events mentioned in this volume of The Emergence of Man appear in bold type). The chart is not to scale; the reason is made clear by the bar below, which represents in linear scale the 4,500 million years spanned by the chart—on the scaled bar, the portion relating to the total period of known human existence (*far right*) is too small to be distinguished.

Geology	Archaeology	Years B.C.	
olocene *ont.)*	**Neolithic** New Stone Age	9000	
			Sheep domesticated in Middle East
			Dog domesticated in North America
		8000	Jericho, oldest known city, settled
			Goat domesticated in Persia
			Man cultivates his first crops, wheat and barley, in Middle East
		7000	Pattern of village life grows in Middle East
			Catal Hüyük, in what is now Turkey, becomes largest Neolithic city
			Loom invented in Middle East
			Cattle domesticated in Middle East
		6000	Agriculture begins to replace hunting in Europe
			Copper used in trade in Mediterranean area
	Copper Age		Corn cultivated in Mexico
		4800	Oldest known massive stone monument built in Brittany
		4000	Sail-propelled boats used in Egypt
			First city-states develop in Sumer
			Cylinder seals begin to be used as marks of identification in Middle East
		3500	First potatoes grown in South America
			Wheel originates in Sumer
			Man begins to cultivate rice in Far East
			Silk moth domesticated in China
			Horse domesticated in south Russia
			Egyptian merchant trading ships start to ply the Mediterranean
			Pictograph writing invented in Middle East
		3000	Bronze first used to make tools in Middle East
			City life spreads to Nile Valley
	Bronze Age		Plough is developed in Middle East
			Accurate calendar based on stellar observation devised in Egypt
		2800	Stonehenge, most famous of ancient stone monuments, begun in England
			Pyramids built in Egypt
			Minoan navigators begin to venture into seas beyond the Mediterranean

Geology	Archaeology	Years B.C.	
Holocene *(cont.)*	**Bronze Age** *(cont.)*	2600	Variety of gods and heroes glorified in *Gilgamesh* and other epics in Middle East
		2500	Cities rise in the Indus Valley
			Earliest evidence of use of skis in Scandinavia
			Earliest written code of laws drawn up in Sumer
		2000	Use of bronze in Europe
			Chicken and elephant domesticated in Indus Valley
			Eskimo culture begins in Bering Strait area
		1500	Invention of ocean-going outrigger canoes enables man to reach islands of South Pacific
			Ceremonial bronze sculptures created in China
			Imperial government, ruling distant provinces, established by Hittites
		1400	Iron in use in Middle East
			First complete alphabet devised in script of the Ugarit people in Syria
			Hebrews introduce concept of monotheism
	Iron Age	1000	Reindeer domesticated in Eurasia
			Phoenicians spread alphabet
		900	
		800	Use of iron begins to spread throughout Europe
			First highway system built in Assyria
			Homer composes *Iliad* and *Odyssey*
			Mounted nomads appear in the Middle East as a new and powerful force
		700	Rome founded
			Wheel barrow invented in China
		200	Epics about India's gods and heroes, the *Mahabharata* and *Ramayana*, written
			Water wheel invented in Middle East
		0	Christian era begins

▼ Two thousand million years ago

▼ One thousand million years ago

First oxygen-breathing animals (900 million)▲

First animals to possess ▲ backbones (470 million)

First men (1.3 million)▲

Credits

The sources for the illustrations in this book are shown below. Credits from left to right are separated by semicolons, from top to bottom by dashes.

Cover—Painting by Burt Silverman, background photograph by Fritz Goro for LIFE. 8—Edward S. Curtis, Philadelphia Museum of Art: Purchased with funds from The American Museum of Photography. 12—Photographed by Robert R. Wright, Denver Museum of Natural History. 14—David Sanger; National Museums of Canada, Ottawa. 16 to 20—Maps by Rafael D. Palacios. 23 to 33—Paintings by Burt Silverman, background photographs are listed separately: 23—ENTHEOS. 24,25—Fritz Goro for LIFE. 26,27—Pete K. Martin. 28,29—ENTHEOS. 30,31—ENTHEOS; John J. Burns. 32,33—ENTHEOS. 34—Walter Barnes courtesy of the Texas Memorial Museum. 38,39—Paintings by Jerome Kuhl. 41—From *Prehistory of North America* by Jesse D. Jennings (After Webb, 1946). Copyright 1968, McGraw-Hill. Used with permission of McGraw-Hill Book Company. Adapted by Roger Hane; Drawings by Nicholas Fasciano. 42,43—Paintings by Roger Hane. 44 to 53—Paintings by Nicholas Fasciano. 54—Courtesy Utah Museum of Natural History, University of Utah, Salt Lake City. 60,61—Lee Boltin courtesy Museum of the American Indian, Heye Foundation. 62—Lee Boltin courtesy Museum of the American Indian, Heye Foundation; Lee Boltin courtesy Smithsonian Institution—Lee Boltin courtesy Museum of the American Indian, Heye Foundation. 64,65—Lee Boltin courtesy Museum of the American Indian, Heye Foundation; Lee Boltin courtesy Smithsonian Institution—Lee Boltin courtesy Museum of the American Indian, Heye Foundation—Lee Boltin courtesy Smithsonian Institution. 69—Lee Boltin courtesy of The American Museum of Natural History. 72,73,74—Paintings by Nicholas Fasciano. 77—Edward S. Curtis copied by Richard Henry courtesy Rare Book Division, The New York Public Library, Astor, Lenox and Tilden Foundations. 78—British Columbia Provincial Museum. 79—Edward S. Curtis, copied by Richard Henry courtesy Rare Book Division, The New York Public Library, Astor, Lenox and Tilden Foundations. 80,81—Reproduced through the courtesy of the Bancroft Library, University of California, Berkeley. 82,83—Provincial Archives, Victoria, British Columbia, courtesy Ralph Andrews. 84—Reproduced through the courtesy of the Bancroft Library, University of California, Berkeley. 85—British Columbia Provincial Museum. 86,87—Edward S. Curtis, copied by Richard Henry courtesy Rare Book Division, The New York Public Library, Astor, Lenox and Tilden Foundations. 88—Stefansson Collection, Dartmouth College Library. 90—Lee Boltin courtesy of The American Museum of Natural History, except centre, courtesy The Robert & Frances Flaherty Study Center, Brattleboro, Vermont. 93—Lee Boltin courtesy of The American Museum of Natural History; National Museums of Canada, Ottawa. 95—Lee Boltin courtesy of The American Museum of Natural History, except centre, National Museums of Canada, Ottawa. 97—Lee Boltin courtesy of The American Museum of Natural History—Stefansson Collection, Dartmouth College Library; Lee Boltin courtesy of The American Museum of Natural History. 98—Fritz Goro for LIFE—Lee Boltin courtesy of The American Museum of Natural History. 100,101—Lee Boltin courtesy of The American Museum of Natural History—W. Thalbitzer photograph, Copyright: Arktisk Institut, Charlottenlund, Denmark; Gontran de Poncins. 102—Lee Boltin courtesy of The American Museum of Natural History, except centre, Robert J. Flaherty photograph courtesy The Museum of Modern Art/Film Stills Archive. 104,105—Fritz Goro for LIFE; Jette Bang photograph, Copyright: Arktisk Institut, Charlottenlund, Denmark—Lee Boltin courtesy of The American Museum of Natural History. 106,107—Lee Boltin courtesy of The American Museum of Natural History—National Museums of Canada, Ottawa; Annan Photo Features—Lee Boltin courtesy of The American Museum of Natural History. 108—Lee Boltin courtesy of The American Museum of Natural History; Gontran de Poncins; Paulus Leeser courtesy Peabody Museum of Archaeology and Ethnology, Harvard University—Lee Boltin courtesy of The American Museum of Natural History. 110—Courtesy Arizona State Museum, The University of Arizona, Helga Teiwes, photographer. 116—From *Prehistory of North America* by Jesse D. Jennings (After Judd, 1964). Copyright 1968, McGraw-Hill. Used with permission of McGraw-Hill Book Company. 118,119—William R. Current. 122—From *The Architecture of Pueblo Bonito* by Neil M. Judd. Smithsonian Miscellaneous Collections, Vol. 147, No. 1. Reprinted by permission of the Smithsonian Institution. Adapted by George V. Kelvin. 123—From *Prehistory of North America* by Jesse D. Jennings (After Judd, 1964). Copyright 1968, McGraw-Hill. Used with permission of McGraw-Hill Book Company. 126 to 128—Paulus Leeser courtesy The Ohio Historical Society, Columbus. 130—Leo Johnson courtesy Milwaukee Public Museum. 134,135—Benschneider courtesy Thomas Gilcrease Institute of American History and Art, Tulsa, Oklahoma. 136,137—Paulus Leeser courtesy Thruston Collection, Vanderbilt University, Nashville. 139—Benschneider courtesy Stovall Museum of Science and History, University of Oklahoma, Norman. 140—Tony Linck. 142—Painting by Victor Lazzaro. 147 to 153—Engravings by Theodore de Bry, after the paintings of Jacques le Moyne de Morgues, courtesy Rare Book Division, The New York Public Library, Astor, Lenox and Tilden Foundations. Photographs copied by Richard Henry appear on the following pages: 147, 148 right, 150 top and bottom right, 151, 152 bottom, and 153.

Acknowledgments

For the help given in the preparation of this book, the editors are particularly indebted to David M. Hopkins, Research Geologist, U.S. Geological Survey, Menlo Park, California, and Joe Ben Wheat, Curator of Anthropology and Professor of Natural History, University of Colorado Museum, Boulder. The editors also express their gratitude to James Anderson, Curator, Cahokia Mound State Park, Cahokia, Illinois; Maud D. Cole, First Assistant, and Lewis M. Stark, Chief, Rare Book Division, The New York Public Library, New York City; Frederick J. Dockstader, Director, Museum of the American Indian, Heye Foundation, New York City; Wilson Duff, Professor of Anthropology, University of British Columbia, Vancouver; Katherine Edsall, Chief Archivist and Katherine Wentworth Rinne, Chief Cataloger, Peabody Museum of Archaeology and Ethnology, Harvard University; Rhodes W. Fairbridge, Professor of Geology, Columbia University; Franklin Folsom, Ward, Colorado; Philip C. Gifford, Department of Anthropology, American Museum of Natural History, New York City; the staff of Thomas Gilcrease Institute of American History and Art, Tulsa, Oklahoma; Donald H. Hiser, City Archaeologist, Director, Pueblo Grande Museum, Phoenix, Arizona; Willard E. Ireland, Provincial Librarian and Archivist, Provincial Archives, Victoria, British Columbia; Jesse D. Jennings, Professor of Anthropology, University of Utah, Salt Lake City; Christopher W. Kirby, Retrieval Advisor, Information Retrieval Section, Office Services Division, National Museums of Canada, Ottawa; William S. Laughlin, Professor, Dept. of Biobehavioral Sciences, University of Connecticut, Storrs; Jerald T. Milanich, Visiting Assistant Professor of Anthropology, University of Florida, Gainesville; Martha P. Otto, Associate Curator, and Elizabeth A. Scheurer, Assistant Curator, Archaeology Division, The Ohio Historical Society, Columbus; Charles A. Repenning, U.S. Geological Survey, Menlo Park, California; Richard H. Tedford, Curator, Department of Vertebrate Palaeontology, American Museum of

Natural History, New York City; David Hurst Thomas, Assistant Curator of North American Archaeology, American Museum of Natural History, New York City; John Barr Tompkins, Curator, Pictorial Collections, The Bancroft Library, University of California, Berkeley; Robert B. Weeden, Professor of Wildlife Man-agement, University of Alaska, Fairbanks; U. Vincent Wilcox III, Curator, Research Branch, Museum of the American Indian, Heye Foundation, New York City; Holly R. Woelke, Assistant Curator of Collections, Arizona State Museum, University of Arizona, Tucson; H. M. Wormington, Research Asso-ciate in Anthropology, University of Colorado Museum and Adjunct Professor of Anthropology, Colorado College, Denver; Walter W. Wright, Chief of Special Collections, Dartmouth College Library, Hanover, New Hampshire.

Bibliography

Caldwell, Joseph R., and Robert L. Hall, eds., *Hopewellian Studies*. Illinois State Museum, 1970.

Dockstader, Frederick J., *Indian Art in America*. New York Graphic Society, 1966.

Driver, Harold E., *Indians of North America*, University of Chicago Press, 1969.

Drucker, Philip, *Indians of the Northwest Coast*. American Museum Science Books, 1955.

Ford, James A., *Eskimo Prehistory in the Vicinity of Point Barrow, Alaska*. Anthropological Papers of The American Museum of Natural History, Vol. 47: Part I, 1959.

Fowler, Melvin L., ed., *Explorations into Cahokia Archaeology*. Illinois Archaeological Survey, Inc., 1969.

Giddings, J. Louis, *Ancient Men of the Arctic*. Alfred A. Knopf, 1967.

Hopkins, David M., ed., *The Bering Land Bridge*, Stanford University Press, 1968.

Jennings, Jesse D., *Prehistory of North America*. McGraw-Hill, 1968.

Martin, P. S., and H. E. Wright Jr., *Pleistocene Extinction: The Search for a Cause*. Yale University Press, 1967.

Mason, Otis Tufton, *Aboriginal American Basketry*. Smithsonian Institution, 1902.

Owen, Roger C., James, J. F., Deetz and Fisher, Anthony D., eds., *The North American Indians*. Collier-Macmillan, 1967.

Silverberg, Robert, *Mound Builders of Ancient America*. New York Graphic Society, 1968.

Spencer, Robert F., and Jennings, Jesse D., eds., *The Native Americans*, Harper and Row, 1965.

Weyer, Edward Moffat, Jr., *The Eskimos, Their Environment and Folkways*. Yale University Press, 1932.

Willey, Gordon R., *An Introduction to American Archaeology*, Vol. 1. Prentice-Hall, 1966.

Wormington, H. M., *Ancient Man in North America*. The Denver Museum of Natural History, 1957.

Index

XXXX
Filmsetting by C. E. Dawkins (Typesetters) Ltd., London, SE1 1UN
Printed and bound in Belgium by Brepols Fabrieken N.V.